Handbook of Reptiles and Amphibians of Florida

PART ONE **THE SNAKES**

by
Ray E. Ashton, Jr. and Patricia Sawyer Ashton

Drawings by René

DATE DUE

Windward Publishing, Inc.

105 NE 25th St.   P.O. Box 371005   Miami, FL 33137

We dedicate this book to the memory of one of the fathers of modern herpetology, Dr. Edward H. Taylor and to all the budding naturalists that may someday study in the field of herpetology.

Second Edition

CONTENTS

ACKNOWLEDGMENTS

The authors wish to express their sincere thanks to the following persons for critically reviewing parts of the manuscript and offering invaluable advice and information: Walter Auffenberg, the late Archie F. Carr, Roger Conant, John E. Cooper, David M. Deitz, Richard Franz, Dale Jackson, John Iverson, Robert Mount, Wilfred T. Neill, William Palmer, Douglas Simmons, and Paul Moler.

For their willingness to provide us with geographic information or data otherwise unavailable, our thanks go the following: the late Ross Allen, David Auth, Alvin Braswell, Gary Bravo, the late Howard "Duke" Campbell, Steve Christman, J. T. Collins, James Dixon, Neil H. Douglas, William E. Duellman, Harold Dundee, Lewis Ehrhart, Thomas Fritz, Patricia G. Hardline, Donald Hoffmeister, Arnold G. Kluge, Gopher Kuntz, David Lee, Alan E. Leviton, Barry Mansell, C. J. McCoy, D. Bruce Means, Peter and Ann Meylan, M. C. Mullen, Peter Pritchard, Douglas Rossman, Stanley Roth, Peter Sachs, William Saunders, Sylvia Scudder, L.H.S. Van Mierop, Charles Wharton, John O. Whittaker, Jr., Kenneth Williams, George Zug, and Richard C. Zweifel.

We are also grateful for the artwork provided by Renaldo Kuhler and for the work submitted by the many photographers for use in this book. Our thanks also go to Annee Moxley for her help in the preparation of the materials and the manuscript.

4

PREFACE

Florida has the richest concentration of reptile and amphibian fauna of any state in this country. Its geographic location, climate, varied physiography, and diversity of habitats support 128 native and approximately 25 introduced species. It is an area where the more northern species meet those of the south and the Caribbean, and the western forms converge on the eastern species. This large hepetofauna has made the state a true haven for amateur and professional herpetologists—those who study reptiles and amphibians.

Herpetologists are not the only people who encounter reptiles and amphibians in Florida. Sportsmen in search of record-breaking bass, bird watchers seeking exotic bird life, or every-day tourists are likely to meet at least one famous reptile during their visit to the state, the American alligator. This spectacular animal is as much a symbol of Florida as are its renowned oranges and famous beaches. In no other state has a reptile attracted so much attention and had so much impact on tourism as the 'gator has in Florida. Each year many thousands of people visit such famous attractions as Ross Allen's Reptile Institute at Silver Springs, which has long featured the alligator in its exhibits and shows.

In addition to alligators, many species of reptiles and amphibians are extremely common and can be seen even in metropolitan areas. The anole inhabits many yards and gardens in the state. New subdivisions, continuously encroaching on once wild areas, include a large array of Florida reptiles and amphibians, often to the dismay of the human inhabitants.

This book has been developed not only for herpetologists, but for those people who visit or live in Florida and are curious about these unusual creatures. It is also intended for students in life sciences, in hopes of providing information about these often misunderstood, feared, and persecuted animals that will lead to a better understanding of their importance in nature.

Towards these ends, an attempt has been made to simplify the scientific information, to limit the use of technical terms, and to write for people with little or no training in biology. We have, further, tried to answer some of the questions that we know from experience are most often asked by the public.

—R.E.A., Jr. and P.S.A.

HERPETOLOGY IN FLORIDA

In no other state in the country have reptiles and amphibians played so prominent a role in history and development as they have in Florida. For more than thirty years visitors to the state have visited Ross Allen's famous Reptile Institute in Silver Springs. Newspapers, television, and a number of books and movies have contained accounts of Ross Allen and his exploits with diamondback rattlesnakes and alligators. Some of the early Tarzan films were made at the Institute, and much of the money provided by the public was used to fund studies by Allen, Wilfred T. Neill, and other herpetologists. The discoveries of these herpetologists attracted numerous others from around the country, and Florida became a mecca for collectors anxious to explore the unique habitats and study their spectacular faunas.

Many visitors eventually came to Florida to study amphibians and reptiles, drawn by less public but even more prominent herpetologists like Archie Carr, famous for his work with sea turtles, Coleman Goin, and others. Earlier herpetological pioneers like Van Hyning, R. F. Deckert, and Thomas Barbour, were the first to make detailed reports on the unique herpetofauna found in the state.

Today, the list of prominent scientists working on amphibians and reptiles in Florida grows, with such herpetologists as Walter Auffenberg, studying subjects like reptilian fossils and gopher tortoises; the late Howard W. Campbell, who researched crocodilians and a variety of snake species; Steve Christman, who is studying faunal distributions; Joan Diemer who has contributed a great wealth of information on gopher tortoises; D. Bruce Means, who is studying the herpetofauna of the panhandle; Roy McDiarmid, who studies numerous species of amphibians and reptiles; Peter Pritchard, who is an expert on turtles; I. Jack Stout and Henry Mushinsky who are contributing to our knowledge of upland species; Richard Franz and Ken Dodd, studying snake behavior; Llewellyn Ehrhart, who has contributed to studies on Florida's sea turtles; Dale Jackson who studies Florida turtles and is doing much to preserve habitat for the state's herpetofauna; Al Schwartz, Tom Hines, and Larry Wilson, studying a broad spectrum of subjects from Caribbean distributions to rattlesnakes.

Researchers in the field who have studied in Florida but have gone elsewhere to continue their studies include Charles Myers, American Museum of Natural History; Robert Mount, Auburn University; Sam Telford, Jr.; Douglas Rossman, Louisiana State University; William E. Duellman, University of Kansas; Charles Wharton, University of Georgia; Wayne King, Bronx Zoological Gardens, now at the Florida State Museum; and John Crenshaw, Georgia Institute of Technology, just to name a few.

Today many students are actively studying Florida amphibians and reptiles. It will become obvious in the species accounts that there are many things that are

6   Herpetology in Florida

unknown and many questions yet to be answered about the state's herpetofauna. We know very little about the day-to-day habits of most species, and virtually nothing about the types of microhabitats required by most species. The little information available on reproduction in many species is only based on captives.

Many worthwhile observations can be made on captive animals if high standards of accuracy are maintained. Information on growth rates, the number, size and weight of young or eggs, breeding, courtship, and longevity are just a few of the types of data that can be obtained. Observations should be recorded on a specimen chart also containing the field collection number, collection date and locality, feeding dates, shedding dates, and other observations.

Field observations on reptiles and amphibians are very difficult and time consuming. One reason why these studies are so difficult is our inability to locate the animal subjects except at certain times. Recently, the development of tiny radio transmitters and the use of radioactive tagging techniques have helped with this major problem. These techniques permit the investigator to locate the animal when it would normally be impossible to find. Once located, observations can be made on microhabitat preferences and the behavior of the animal.

The kinds of information mentioned above and in depth natural history studies conducted in the field are critically important to any type of conservation effort. Without knowledge of specific habitat requirements and the behavior of threatened or endangered animals, conservation efforts can only be superficial at best.

There are still many unanswered questions about the taxonomic relationships of many species. The kingsnakes, crowned and water snakes, and chorus frogs are just a few groups that are in need of further study.

CONSERVATION

Before the environmental awareness of the 1960's alerted many people to the serious plight of our natural environments and all their inhabitants, most conservationists were mainly concerned about the potential extinction of some birds, mammals, and a few species of fish. Little attention was paid to the plight of reptiles and amphibians. Today, an ever growing list of reptiles and amphibians and their critical habitats are being protected by state and federal laws.

To some people, the increased number of laws governing collecting, maintaining, studying, and importing reptiles and amphibians may seem overly restrictive, serving mostly to supress interest in herpetology on the part of our young people. However, less than 10% of our native reptiles and amphibians are protected; the remainder can be collected and studied without concern for legal restrictions. Many protected species are those that have been the victims of massive habitat destruction and are now limited to only a small percent of their original range. This destruction is the result of land development for agriculture, lumbering, and homesites, and has been so rapid and massive in some areas that the natural habitat has all but disappeared completely. Those natural areas that remain are being increasingly assaulted by masses of people with overland vehicles and dirt bikes, and by camper ghettos, whose occupants move in with little knowledge of, or concern for, the habitats and the living heritage which they contain. Many of them are especially contemptuous of amphibians and reptiles, not hesitating to slaughter harmless and poisonous snakes alike, or to take target practice on sunning turtles or frogs in a pond or lake. To make things worse, some game protectors and other law enforcement officials are unwilling to halt such practices.

Herpetologists, amateurs and professionals alike, can help in the battle to save at least a few islands of natural habitat by educating the general public and increasing their awareness. This can be done by visiting schools, scout troops, and other organizations, using attractive photographs and informing the audiences of the aesthetic appeal and ecological value of these animals. Contempt and disinterest must be converted into curiosity and respect. If more naturalists don't join these endeavors soon, the number of species and their critical habitats that will require protective measures will increase drastically.

Collectors should also maintain a strong conservation ethic in their own herpetological activities. Over-collecting or destroying the habitat can have a drastic effect on local amphibian and reptile populations. Take only those individuals and species as you have a need for and don't collect specimens to sell in the pet trade. Often it is a greater challenge to photograph an animal in its natural habitat than it is to collect it. Finally, don't release exotic species into Florida habitats—the long term effects on native species could be catastrophic.

HERPETOLOGY AND THE LAW

Several state laws relate to collecting and maintaining reptiles and amphibians in Florida. Specific information can be obtained by contacting local game authorities or by writing the Florida Game and Freshwater Fish Commission, Farris Bryant Building, 620 South Meridian Street, Tallahassee, Florida 32304.

Persons interested in collecting or maintaining protected reptiles and amphibians for research or educational purposes can apply for a scientific collecting permit. This permit is issued on a calendar year basis, and, at the end of the year, a report of collections made must be filed. Young resident Floridians and other Florida amateurs intending to collect or keep a few of the unprotected native reptiles or amphibians for their own study, and not for sale, do not, as the law now stands, need a collecting permit. Out of state visitors, including amateurs, intending to collect in Florida should apply for a permit several months in advance of their collecting trip. Special permits are needed for displaying reptiles or amphibians, and a bond is required for maintaining poisonous reptiles in captivity. Permits do not allow the taking of threatened or endangered species, which include the indigo snake, pine barrens treefrog, American crocodile, all sea turtles, and others. Other animals are protected from export or sale, including the gopher tortoise, alligator snapping turtle, and Barbour's map turtle. A special permit is required to possess any gopher tortoises in the state of Florida.

The Endangered Species Act of 1973 protects the American crocodile, pine barrens treefrog, Atlantic hawksbill, Atlantic ridley, Atlantic leatherback, indigo snake, Atlantic salt marsh snake, Atlantic green turtle, Atlantic loggerhead turtle, and alligator, which has since been changed to protected species. Several other Florida species are being considered for protection under this act including the short-tailed snake, rim rock crowned snake, and key mud turtle. Others will undoubtedly follow. For details of the federal endangered species law or other pertinent laws, or for information concerning permits to take or study these protected animals, write U.S. Fish and Wildlife Service, P.O. Box 95467, Atlanta, GA, 30347.

Importation of certain reptiles and amphibians into the United States from foreign countries is restricted by international treaties, the federal Lacey Act, and the CITES treaty. Before importing exotic species, check with the U.S. Fish and Wildlife Service or with customs officials at Miami International Airport.

There are also state and federal laws against the release of exotic species into the state. Only the Florida Game and Freshwater Fish Commission has the authority to release non-native species in the state.

THE LANGUAGE OF SCIENCE: INTERPRETING TERMINOLOGY AND CLASSIFICATION

Just as we need a name, address, state, and zip code for the postman to locate and deliver a letter to a specific individual among the millions who live in this vast country, scientists need a system to identify individual plant and animal species among the approximately 2 million different species thought to now inhabit the earth. Being able to name and locate individual species does not necessarily indicate the relationships of these species to each other. Locating all the Smiths in the phone book of one town does not tell you if they are related. Just as tracing human geneaology is a complex and often confusing process, so is the system of biological classification, but just as curiosity and often legal necessity causes us to seek our roots amid the complexities of geneaology, the scientist, in order to better understand the biological world, must deal with systems of classification.

HISTORY

The process of developing a usable biological classification system goes back to the ancient Greeks, Aristotle and Theophrastus. Organisms were then classified based on similarity of appearance, or on where they lived. Later in the Middle Ages "beastiaries" and "herbals" classified organisms according to their usefullness to man. Many classification systems have been used throughout history but the Swedish scientist Carl von Linné (Linnaeus) set forth a system in his work *Systema Naturae (Classification of Nature)* in 1737 which was the forerunner of the system in use today. Linnaeus grouped organisms according to similarity of structure. He placed all organisms which appeared built alike in the same species and grouped those species which were similar into the same genus. In other words, he placed all horses in the same species and horses and donkeys were in the same genus. Groups of similar genera can then be grouped together into still larger categories.

While our present system of classification was spawned by Linnaeus, certain differences exist. Visible structural similarity alone has been found to be insufficient for accurate classification so many more factors are considered today. Genetics has lent new dimensions to the system of classification. Scientists often disagree on species distinctions and the way an organism is classified may change as new studies reveal additional information. Linnaeus saw

Interpreting Terminology and Classification

each species as an unchanging, fixed form of life, each member of which was identical in basic structure. The modern view now includes information gained from evolutionary theory and from evidence that there exists a range of natural variation within populations of species. Unlike Linnaeus, modern scientists do not now assume that visual differences necessarily mean different species. Just as few humans look exactly alike, no two members of the same species need appear precisely identical.

SCIENTIFIC NAMES

Linnaeus gave each individual, structurally identical group of organisms a binomial designation (a two-part name), which we now call a scientific name, consisting of two parts, the genus and species. The scientific name of an organism, unlike a common name, is given only to that particular organism and is recognized world wide, regardless of the native language of the person reading it, since all scientific names are in a latinized form, usually composed from Latin or Greek roots. The genus name is always capitalized while the species name is not. Both names are underlined unless they are italicized. When repeating a genus name, the genus may be represented by only the capitalized first letter: e.g., *Nerodia fasciata, N. fasciata, N. taxispilota.* Even though not spelled out the last two names both mean that the genus is *Nerodia (N).*

Rules of scientific nomenclature are established by international congresses. Scientists strive to follow these rules. However, rules change, and new knowledge is discovered which may change previously believed relationships of organisms so don't be surprised if texts from different times in history, and even contemporary or future works, use different scientific names or classifications for the same organism. These changes are, however, carefully recorded according to specific rules so that the changes can be traced. Entire books are devoted to listing the synonomies, or other scientific names by which particular organisms have been called.

CLASSIFICATION SYSTEM

The categories of classification which are in use today, beginning with the largest grouping, are KINGDOM, PHYLUM, CLASS, ORDER, FAMILY, GENUS, and SPECIES. Intermediate groupings such as subphylum or subspecies are sometimes inserted. When subspecies names are used the scientific name may have three parts instead of two as in *Nerodia fasciata clarki.*

All snakes are in the kingdom—animalia, phylum—chordata, and class—reptilia. Snakes share the kingdom animalia with all other animals, and the phylum chordata with all fishes, amphibians, other reptiles, birds and mammals, and the class reptilia with the lizards, turtles, and crocodilians. Classes such as reptilia are further divided into orders and the snakes occupy the order squamata which includes both snakes and lizards, and the suborder serpentes, the snakes. Orders are further divided into families which are described later in this book (see family accounts). Families are divided into genera, and genera into species.

HOW TO USE THIS BOOK

This book is designed to provide an easy method of identifying the snakes found in Florida. By following the easy steps, even a beginner should be able to accurately identify most species.

To identify a specimen, first of all simply leaf through the pictures until you find one resembling your snake. Read the description, check the key character diagrams, and make note of the habitat and range, comparing them to the location your specimen is from. If the habitat and range do not match, it does not necessarily mean that your specimen is not that species, but it would be wise to continue looking at other species in the book, until all possibilities are exhausted. If you have collected a snake from an area not already marked as part of its range, the specimen and proper collection data would be useful to a museum or university keeping specimens from Florida. (Refer to pages 37, 56.) After identifying your snake, you may wish to place a check by its name in the habitat where it was found on the Species Habitat Chart, pages 48-51.

If you are interested in collecting a particular species, you should read the account and then turn to the Species Habitat Chart to determine the most likely places to find the snake. The section on habitats will be useful in understanding the meaning of the habitat titles.

THE FLORIDA ENVIRONMENT

The state of Florida, covering approximately 58,560 square miles, offers a variety of habitats for reptiles and amphibians. These habitats are the result of, and are affected by, geologic history, climate, and man's influence.

The Florida peninsula, presently extending from 24.6° to 31° north latitude and from 80° to 87.6° west longitude, has existed as part of a much broader area called the Floridian Plateau since the early Cretaceous period—about 134 million years ago. From the Cretaceous through the Oligocene, the peninsula was separated from the mainland by a seaway, and floodings during the Eocene and Oligocene deposited vast layers of limestone. By the Miocene (25 million years ago) modern Florida made its appearance as a small coral island. More of Florida continued to emerge and it became connected to the continental land mass during the

The Florida Environment

Pliocene, some ten million years ago. Sea level fluctuations during the glacial periods of the Pleistocene (1 million years ago) again submerged much of the Florida peninsula and the receding seas left more deposits. These various sediment depositions have given Florida a great variety of soil types, which in turn support a variety of habitats.

So we see that Florida is a physiographically young state with the southern region of very flat land having been above sea level only since the Pleistocene, and some of the eastern coast emerging even more recently. The coastal topography of Florida consists mainly of gently sloping marine terraces which are characterized by a lack of relief resulting in poor drainage. Inland, the largest south Florida lake, Lake Okeechobee, is surrounded by flat marshlands which extend southward into the area known as the Everglades. North of Lake Okeechobee is a hilly region with few areas more than 125 feet (38 m) above sea level, the exception being the Highlands County lake region. Central Florida contains some very hilly areas with elevations as high as 324 feet (98 m) above sea level near Lake Wales in Polk County. Central and north-central Florida are known for their karst topography. Here, the limestone deposited in the geologic past lies close to the surface. The action of water containing dissolved CO_2 on the limestone creates a soluble product that can be carried off. As a result, the limestone is gradually eaten away forming underground waterways, and, where the surface collapses, sinkholes, sinkhole lakes, and caves. As we move north, streams become more frequent and deeper. The northeastern areas contain some freshwater marshlands and again the coastal borders are low and flat, including some saltwater marshes. As you move westward, the topography and soils vary, ranging from the limestone caves at Marianna and the red clays of the Tallahassee region to the white sands and salt marshes of the gulf coastal beaches. On the whole, Florida is drained by a series of rivers, but a central ridge divides the drainage of the peninsula, east from west. Not incidentally should be mentioned the Florida Keys, a series of islands off the tip of Florida. They extend about 135 miles (217 km) south of the mainland and are part of Monroe County, Florida.

Florida is generally known for its southern subtropical and tropical climates. The northern third of the state is warm and temperate. Weather throughout the state is considered mild, especially the weather along the east coast which is tempered by the proximity of the Gulf Stream.

Coastal regions also experience slightly warmer temperatures in the winter and cooler in the summer than inland regions at the same latitude. The mean annual temperature in Florida is in the 70's (20's in degrees Celsius), and almost no part of the state can be considered frost free, though the extreme southern tip of the state and the keys rarely experience freezing temperatures. This may account for the survival and establishment of some tropical species in those southern areas. The rainy season in Florida generally occurs from June to October. Almost all of Florida's precipitation occurs as rain, though it has been known to snow in all parts of the state.

Florida generally has a high relative humidity, because most of the wind patterns which affect Florida must pass over water. Gentle breezes occur almost

The Florida Environment

daily in all places during summer. The prevailing winds come from the east and southeast. Hurricanes generally occur in late summer and early fall and can catastrophically alter Florida habitats.

Man has had an even more catastrophic effect on Florida's natural habitats than hurricanes. A hurricane's effect may only be temporary; eventually, natural succession will return the land to its former state. Man's damage is often far reaching and irreparable. Man has altered the atmosphere and waterways with his chemical wastes and has altered the landscape with his pastures, farmlands, buildings, highways, canals and monoculture timberlands. He has wiped out native species and has introduced new ones. The recent introduction of various exotic plants and animals has created problems that were not foreseen. Prime examples are the water hyacinth and hydrilla which choke waterways, and the Australian pine, *Casuarina,* which now thrives and forces out many natural species in south Florida. Recently introduced fish species threaten to displace many of our more desirable game fish. Once gone, the lost species or habitats cannot be replaced. Habitat destruction can occur both directly and indirectly. Habitats may be cut over, built on, or polluted chemically. They can also be destroyed by surrounding them with concrete pavement and buildings which alter wind, temperature, and drainage patterns. Pollution of underground waterways with chemicals and biological wastes can affect habitats hundreds of miles away. Highways and buildings can affect animal populations by cutting across natural migration routes, destroying seasonal breeding grounds or cutting off food supplies.

FLORIDA HABITATS

There are many ways to describe and delineate habitats. We have chosen to divide them into general categories which best reflect differences in suitability for reptiles and amphibians, based on such characters as moisture and type of cover. The habitats roughly correspond to the plant communities for which they are named. Our habitat categories are very broad and by no means describe all the specific plant communities of the state.

The most obvious division of habitats is the separation of the aquatic from the terrestrial. In nature, there is generally no clear-cut dividing line, rather, one habitat will blend into another. Aquatic habitats are affected by and affect the terrestrial habitats surrounding them. Certain reptiles or amphibians may occupy an aquatic habitat and the surrounding terrestrial habitats on a regular basis, or only at certain times of the year depending on moisture or breeding season.

The aquatic habitats may be divided as follows: 1. salt marshes, 2. mangrove swamps, 3. freshwater marshes, 4. cypress swamps and domes, 5. gum swamps and river swamps, 6. temporary ponds and roadside ditches, 7. permanent ponds and lakes, 8. small streams and creeks, 9. rivers, and 10. canals. The terrestrial habitats include: 1. pine flatwoods, 2. sand pine-rosemary scrub, 3. longleaf pine-turkey oak sandhills, 4. xeric oak hammocks (dry), 5. mesic hammocks (damp woodland), 6. hydric hammocks (wet woodland), 7. tropical hammocks, 8. temperate deciduous forests, 9. human habitations, golf courses, trash piles, 10. farmlands, fields, disturbed areas, and 11. coastal beaches and dunes.

AQUATIC HABITATS

Salt Marshes: Along the coast of Florida in areas of low relief where freshwater streams or rivers drain gradually into the ocean and mix with the salt water to form waters of varying salinities, salt marshes can be found. This habitat is characterized by plant species which are tolerant of a variety of intermediate stages between salt and fresh water. Salt marshes appear as extensive plain-like grasslands usually dominated by cord grass *(Spartina)* and salt grass *(Distichlis)* in areas regularly flooded by high tides. The more brackish areas, which may only be seasonally flooded, often support dense stands of rushes *(Juncus roemerianus)*. As you move inland into areas where the salt content of the water is lower, the vegetation gradually changes and the salt marsh may eventually merge into a freshwater marsh. Where the salt marsh meets higher ground, the change in vegetation may be abrupt. Islands of trees and dense vegetation may appear to rise up out of the marshy prairie. Deeper channels of open water may wind their way in and out across these grasslands, providing access by boat for the interested explorer. Walking through salt marshes is often quite difficult. The vegetation often has cutting edges or needle sharp points, and the ground generally consists of several feet of mud and decaying vegetation. Salt marshes are most extensive along the southwest and northwest coasts of Florida. In some areas, they may merge with mangrove swamps.

The salinity of the water in the salt marsh habitats presents an insurmountable problem to most amphibians which require freshwater breeding ponds to lay eggs. Some reptiles are able to adapt to this environment and cottonmouths, salt marsh snakes, terrapins, crocodiles, and alligators may be seen.

Mangrove Swamps: Southern Florida coastal areas and much of the Florida keys are known for their mangrove swamps. These, like the salt marsh, form a transition zone between the salt waters of the ocean and the less salty inland habitats. The mangrove swamp is characterized by the well-known red mangrove *(Rhizophora mangle)* with its arching roots, which anchor it in the shifting sands of areas constantly flooded by ocean tides. Areas farther inland that are more frequently out of water may support growths of the black mangrove *(Avicennia nitida)* with its hundreds of tube-like roots rising out of the mud, and of the white mangrove *(Laguncularia racemosa)*. Buttonwood *(Conocarpus erecta)* is another common member of this community and is generally found well above the high tide line. Mangrove swamps are found along the Gulf coast as far north as the Suwannee River, and on the Atlantic coast where they end in northern Brevard County. This fast disappearing habitat forms dense vegetative borders, often merging with salt marshes. The conditions for amphibians and reptiles are similar to the salt marsh community, and the reptile inhabitants are the same as well. However, the woody growth of the mangrove swamp supports a greater diversity, and *Eumeces inexpectatus*, *Anolis*, and *Elaphe guttata* are commonly found.

Freshwater Marshes: Freshwater marshes occur extensively in Florida and are characterized by soils of slow drainage where there is standing fresh water much of the year. There are a number of different plant communities which may dominate the areas termed freshwater marshes. The type of vegetation in any given area may be determined by the fluctuation of the water level in that area. The well-known Everglades are a broad expanse of predominantly freshwater

Florida Habitats

marshes which may be dominated by cattails *(Typha)*, pickerel weed *(Pontederia)*, or maiden cane *(Panicum)*. The associated vegetation of freshwater marshes is too diverse to list, but it includes a variety of small trees, shrubs, grasses, and flowering herbs. Freshwater marshes often have pond-like areas of open water or canals winding through them, providing access by boat. Walking in marshes is a muddy job because of the thick layers of mud and peat held in place by thousands of plant roots. Freshwater marshes may be vast expanses of vegetation, or they may only border a lake or pond. They provide excellent moisture and cover for many reptiles and amphibians. Where the marsh meets higher land and drier habitats, the greatest density and variety of organisms may be found. Reptiles and amphibians may move, according to their needs, to the moisture of the marsh or onto the land and its vegetation. Some turtles, snakes and alligators lay their eggs in the soils of the banks or woodlands. Some frogs, toads, and salamanders move to the waters to lay their eggs, which must remain moist.

Drought and fire are two serious hazards to the marsh. Marshes depend on run-off from surrounding areas, as well as on direct rain, for their water supply. As the state becomes more developed, the drainage patterns are disrupted. Some marshes are intentionally drained to produce more dry land, and others lost their water into man-made canals. Highways, buildings, and canals all interfere with the normal water flow from the surrounding land into freshwater marshes. One of the greatest freshwater marshes, the Everglades, is endangered by the continuing encroachment of civilization. Interference with drainage from Lake Okeechobee into the Everglades has caused serious droughts in recent years. With droughts often come fires. The years of decaying vegetation held in place by the roots of the sawgrass, hold moisture for a considerable period of time. But when dry, this peat along with the dried surface vegetation, can fuel intense fires that can sweep across the Everglades and through the hammock islands and pinelands that dot the horizon here and there in this vast marsh.

Temporary Ponds and Roadside Ditches: Low areas in pine flatwoods, the bottom of shallow sink holes, or any poorly drained depressions may become temporary ponds in time of heavy rains. These ponds are generally dry most of the year but may support heavy amphibian populations when filled. Roadside ditches frequently fill as well during heavy rains, and, as in temporary ponds, the shallow water generally covers a dense growth of water-tolerant vegetation that is out of water much of the year. This vegetation provides excellent cover for breeding amphibians or for reptiles such as water snakes, which feed upon the amphibians.

Permanent Ponds and Lakes: Natural ponds and lakes are more common in the central and northern part of the state than in the south. Surrounding vegetation may vary greatly from grassy marshes to cypress *(Taxodium)* or gum *(Nyssa)* swamps to grassy backyards or cleared sand beaches. The presence of amphibian and reptile populations will depend mainly on the amount of cover available and on the surrounding habitats. Few amphibians or reptiles would be

Juncus marsh

red mangrove swamp

Florida Habitats

WILLIAM B. and KATHLEEN V. LOVE

Everglades

DAVID LEE
RAY E. ASHTON, JR.

roadside ditch

cypress swamp

Florida Habitats

found in the open, deeper waters of the lake. Most would be concentrated in the shallower edge areas with cover. Some lakes or ponds may contain floating aquatic vegetation such as water hyacinth (*Eichhornia crassipes*), water lilies (*Nymphaea ssp.*), water chinquapin (*Nuphar lutea*), or water lettuce (*Pistia stratiotes*). Such vegetation provides additional cover for many amphibians, which may also use the vegetation as convenient perches even far out into the pond or lake. Alligators and water snakes are also frequent inhabitants of ponds and lakes.

Cypress Swamps and Domes: Cypress swamps and domes are freshwater areas dominated by cypress trees (*Taxodium*). The dark, stained waters of these areas are generally shallow, and may dry up during part of the year. In cypress swamps, the muddy ground may support various ferns or hydrophilic plants during the drier periods. Cypress areas (referred to as domes) which tend to be dry for longer periods during the year may support extensive grass and herbaceous floras. When flooded, the grass clumps and other vegetation provide important cover for reptiles and amphibians. Cypress swamps generally cover larger areas than domes. The trees are usually closely spaced, with Spanish moss and other epiphytes hanging from the branches. The dim, eerie light beneath the trees and the occasional open pools of dark water have set the scene for many tales of alligators and water moccasins. Cypress domes on the other hand are generally less extensive than swamps. They are roughly circular stands of trees which, if viewed from a distance, form a dome-shaped outline against the horizon. Due to heavy logging of cypress, many of these areas contain stumps and felled trees which form excellent cover for reptiles and amphibians. The shallow water and cover available in cypress areas provide seasonal breeding grounds for many amphibians and reptiles.

Gum Swamps and River Swamps: Located on river flood plains or bottomlands, gum swamps or river swamps are dominated by gum or tupelo trees (*Nyssa*), and may contain titi (*Cyrilla racemiflora*), sweetbay (*Magnolia virginiana*), and a variety of other trees and shrubs which are tolerant of poorly drained soils or soils that are seasonally flooded. Dense undergrowth and shade predominate in this habitat. Conditions generally range from moist to very wet throughout the year, which makes this an ideal habitat for many amphibians and snakes which feed on them.

Rivers: Florida is drained by several river systems which are chiefly separated east from west by a high central Florida ridge. Some of the better known river systems include the Suwannee, the St. Johns, the Oklawaha, and the Apalachicola. Rivers may serve as boundaries separating one area or species from another or as corridors of dispersal, bringing species from one area into another. As an example, the Suwannee serves the latter function, bringing many Georgia species into its drainage in Florida. Rivers may be bordered by high ground areas, which are generally hardwood hammocks, or by bottomland river swamp. Rivers may be separated from streams and creeks by their size and depth. Rivers in

Florida Habitats

Florida are often fed by crystal clear springs, and the river may run clear for a time before becoming stained by the acids formed by decaying vegetation.

River banks provide nest sites for turtles. Still water and backwash areas provide areas suitable for amphibians to lay their eggs. At the right time of year, journeying down a Florida river in a canoe will usually result in discovery of water snakes sunning in overhanging branches or turtles sunning on logs.

Small Streams and Creeks: Streams and creeks are usually part of a river drainage system, though they may drain swamps, lakes, ponds, or upland areas. Streams generally maintain a constant flow in one direction. In Florida, stream types may vary from having clear spring water to tanin-rich black water. They are generally shallow and rapid moving, and may flow through a variety of terrestrial habitats. They may contain backwash areas or leaf beds providing suitable habitat for many amphibians.

Some streams contain rooted aquatic vegetation such as pond weeds (*Potamogeton*) and wild celery (*Vallisneria*). Many are densely shaded by overhanging vegetation. Tangles of fallen vegetation, or rocks may provide cover in the stream for a variety of reptile and amphibian inhabitants.

Canals: South Florida, in particular, is criss-crossed with a multitude of manmade canals. These canals were made to drain land so that it could be farmed and developed. They are relatively unwholesome environments, offering little to most reptiles or amphibians and containing little diversity of species.

Canal banks are usually still and barren and provide little cover. The water is often silty from run-off and frequently polluted by chemical or biological wastes. Most contain massive growths of slimy algae, bacteria, or waterweeds such as elodea (*Anachris*) or water hyacinth (*Eichhornia crassipes*). Some may contain some rather unusual introduced species of fish. A few frog or turtle species and very often alligators and caimans are found in these rather unwholesome canals. Some canals, containing predominantly floating aquatic vegetation and having some bank cover, are more suitable to reptiles and amphibians. These may contain a profusion of turtles, water snakes, or alligators along with various amphibian species.

cypress dome pond

natural lake

spring fed river

Florida Habitats

stream through mesic hammock

mesic hammock

Florida Habitats

TERRESTRIAL HABITATS

Pine Flatwoods: This habitat is characterized by longleaf pine species (predominantly *Pinus palustris, Pinus serotina,* or *Pinus elliottii)* which occupy land of relatively low relief, usually in areas of poor drainage. Freshwater marsh, pond, or lake habitats may be associated with pine flatwoods, and cypress domes are often scattered as isolated islands throughout the flatwoods. Pine flatwoods generally have well spaced trees with various kinds of understory shrubs. Saw palmetto *(Serenoa repens),* gallberry *(Ilex glabra)* and wax myrtle *(Myrica cerifera)* are the most common. Flatwoods offer a great variety of wild flowers in spring and fall.

Pine flatwoods habitat can also include the monoculture pinewoods planted by man. In monoculture pine, the trees are obviously planted in evenly spaced rows. The understory vegetation is the same as stated above.

Pine flatwoods are a fire adapted community. This means that without fire, the community would, over a period of years, become unsuitable for the species that presently live there. Fire in these communities is a natural occurrence, generally started by lightning before the presence of man. The thick layer of pine needles on the forest floor and the various ground cover fuel a relatively light fire which helps maintain the community by opening up the understory and germinating certain kinds of seeds.

This habitat provides important cover for many amphibians during the part of the year that they are not in breeding ponds. Excellent cover is provided here for reptiles as well.

Sand Pine and Rosemary Scrub: This habitat is dominated by sand pine *(Pinus clausa)* and rosemary *(Ceratiola ericoides).* This plant association is found on light colored, well-drained soils usually on high ground. The trees are widely spaced. The understory is relatively open, and the ground is covered with a variety of low herbs, lichens, and wild flowers. This habitat is most frequent in the center of the state. Standing water is relatively scarce in this habitat, and neither the soil nor vegetation seem to hold much water or produce a high microclimate humidity. Lack of moisture makes amphibians relatively scarce, though some make use of the gopher tortoise burrows, pocket gopher *(Geomys)* burrows, and occasional small ponds in this habitat where the moisture levels are greater. Reptiles are common, including a great variety of lizards, snakes, and, of course, gopher tortoises.

Longleaf Pine-Turkey Oak Sandhills: Dominated by longleaf pine *(Pinus palustris)* and turkey oak *(Quercus laevis),* this community is usually found on high, well-drained, sandy soils. The trees are widely spaced with open grassy areas between. Wire grass *(Aristida stricta)* is the common ground cover. Understory shrubs include saw palmetto *(Serenoa repens),* and pawpaw *(Asimina).* This is also a fire adapted community. Open water is not common. Amphibians may make use of gopher tortoise burrows where the humidity is higher. Reptiles are common where there is good cover.

Florida Habitats

Florida's Changing Pinelands: Both the sand pine-rosemary scrub and the longleaf pine-turkey oak communities have been greatly damaged by man in the state of Florida. Their location on high, dry soils makes them ideal for housing developments and for citrus farming. Much of the virgin pine land of the state had been cut over at least once by 1930. Most pinelands in existence today are areas where pine has regenerated. Citrus groves have replaced many of these pine communities in central and southern Florida. Unfortunately, citrus groves lack the necessary habitat requirements for the reptiles and amphibians that occupied the pine communities, and, consequently, citrus groves support few of them.

Xeric Oak Hammock: Found on relatively dry, sandy soils, that generally were once occupied by pine, the xeric oak hammock is dominated by several species of oak including turkey oak *(Quercus laevis),* blue jack oak *(Quercus incana),* southern red oak *(Quercus falcata),* and live oak *(Quercus virginiana).* The trees are usually well spaced and the ground is generally grassy, with a variety of flowering herbaceous plants in sunny areas. Standing water is uncommon in this habitat, though an occasional shallow pond may be present. Amphibians are less common in this habitat because of the general lack of moisture. A variety of reptiles, including gopher tortoises are present.

Mesic Hammocks (Damp Woodland): This woodland of moderate moisture is characterized by the presence of southern magnolia *(Magnolia grandiflora),* and laurel oak *(Quercus laurifolia),* along with a variety of other tree species including blue-beech *(Carpinus caroliniana),* hophornbeam *(Ostrya virginiana),* flowering dogwood *(Cornus florida),* and American holly *(Ilex opaca).* Typically the mesic hammock has three vegetation layers, an overstory of large tall trees, an understory of smaller trees and shrubs, and the ground cover of grasses, herbaceous plants and lower shrubs. Shade predominates and the vegetation forms tangled thickets tied together by greenbriers *(Smilax)* and grape vines *(Vitis).* Streams may wind through the hammock, or the canopy may open around a small pond. The conditions in the hammock are moderate throughout the year. The dense vegetation protects the hammock from drying winds and from temperature extremes. The moist, moderate conditions are ideal for many reptiles and amphibians.

Hydric Hammock: These low, flat woodlands are subject to periodic flooding. The trees may include a variety of water-hardy species such as water oak *(Quercus nigra),* sweet gum *(Liquadambar styraciflua),* winged elm *(Ulmus alata),* hackberry *(Celtis laevigata),* willow *(Salix nigra),* and box elder *(Acer negundo).* These thick woods surround streams and river bottoms. The habitat is variable; part of the year it is dry with leaf litter on the ground, and then is wet and muddy during other times. This provides ideal habitat in terms of moisture and cover for many reptiles and amphibians.

Tropical Hammock: This category includes a variety of southern Florida hammocks. They are composed mainly of a variety of tropical plant species,

Florida Habitats

pine flatwoods

longleaf pine-turkey oak sandhills, wire grass

xeric oak hammock

Florida Habitats

flatwoods pond

sand pine scrub

Florida Habitats

which form dense canopies of vegetation, and relatively open hammock floor covered with layers of rotting vegetation and ferns. Lianas (large vines) are common and give this habitat its typical "tropical" appearance. Epiphytes (air plants) such as orchids, bromeliads, mosses, and lichens may cover the tree limbs. The tree species include predominantly evergreen, non-coniferous hardwoods such as gumbo-limbo *(Bursera simaruba)*, pigeon-plum *(Coccoloba diversifola)*, mahogany *(Swietenia mahogani)*, poisonwood *(Metopium toxiferum)* and strangler fig *(Ficus aurea)*.

These hammocks may be found as isolated highlands in the middle of wet prairies like the Everglades, or some still remain protected areas along the tip of Florida and on a few keys. They occupy higher limestone outcroppings. Most of this type of habitat has been destroyed by the large scale building in south Florida that started in the 1920's.

This habitat is also endangered in south Florida by the introduction of Australian pine *(Casuarina equisetifolia)* and melaleuca *(Melaleuca)*. These trees have begun to slowly replace the dominant hammock species along hammock borders or where trees have been weakened or destroyed by fire.

Temperate Deciduous Forest: This is the common deciduous forest of the eastern United States, north of Florida. The relief is typically hilly and the soil is well drained. The forest floor is generally covered with a layer of dead leaves and decaying vegetation. In the spring and summer, ferns and wild flowers dot the ground beneath the shade of these broad-leafed trees. Streams may wind through the forest, or the canopy may open onto a field, grassland, or farm pond. The dominant tree species generally include oaks *(Quercus)*, hickories *(Carya)*, elm *(Ulmus)*, maple *(Acer)*, basswood *(Tilia)*, tulip poplar *(Liriodendron tulipifera)*, beech *(Fagus grandifolia)*, and walnuts *(Juglans)*. Temperate deciduous forests are found in northern peninsular Florida and in the pan-handle. The conditions for reptiles are good, particularly where there is good cover such as fallen logs. Amphibians that require water to breed are found near streams or temporary ponds that may form after heavy rains. Salamanders which breed under moist logs and leaf litter may also be found. This habitat is where northern species such as the copperhead make their intrusion into Florida.

Human Habitations, Golf Courses, Trash Piles: In Florida, human developments have produced their own habitats for reptiles and amphibians. Some examples we are all familiar with are the snake in the woodpile, the frog eggs in the bird bath, or the treefrog on the window sill. Lights around buildings and street lamps attract insects, which in turn attract insect eating amphibians such as treefrogs and toads. Golf course lights and ponds provide a perfect combination for frogs and toads—moisture and insect attracting lights.

Another by-product of human existence is trash. Trash piles are unique in their attraction for various reptiles and amphibians. Many articles found on trash piles such as mattresses, refrigerators, sofas, and cardboard boxes hold moisture long after soaking rains, so they provide excellent moisture and cover. A variety of reptiles and amphibians may be found, depending on the habitat surrounding the the trash pile location.

Coastal Beaches and Dunes: Beaches and dunes generally consist of expanses of sand bordered by the ocean on one side and by dune forests, open fields, human habitations, or roads on the other. The type of associated coastal vegetation depends on the location of the particular beach or dune. In general, the vegetation has special adaptations such as waxy, succulent leaves to prevent water loss or secretory glands to eliminate excess salt. Most vegetation must also be adapted to salt spray and possible inundation by salt water. Typical species include sea purslane *(Sesuvium)*, seaside pennywort *(Hydrocotyle bonariensis)*, sea oats *(Uniola paniculata)*, railroad-vine *(Ipomoea)*, camphorplant *(Heterotheca subaxillaris)*, saw palmetto *(Serenoa repens)*, and salt bush *(Baccharis halimifolia)*.

pond surrounded by hydric hammock

strangler fig in tropical hammock

deciduous forest—upper panhandle

Florida Habitats

RAY E. ASHTON, JR.

human habitat—remains of old house

PATRICIA SAWYER ASHTON

coastal dunes and beaches

Florida Habitats

CAPTURING REPTILES

Anyone interested in collecting reptiles should first be certain to learn to identify the poisonous varieties. One way to do this is to study the species accounts and photographs of the venomous snakes in this book. Then visit a zoo or museum where live specimens are on display. Study them until there is no question of your ability to make identifications. Even then, do not handle any snakes that you are not sure of, since such oddities as black coral snakes and copperheads without patterns occasionally turn up.

A second major "rule" of reptile collecting, indeed all animal collecting, is to learn to identify protected species and to leave them alone. If you have legitimate reasons for collecting them, you may be able to obtain a permit from the appropriate state and federal agency to take a certain species. These permits are not issued without good cause, however, and general or commercial collectors will be denied. Some species which are not necessarily designated as protected may have certain restrictions on the numbers which may be taken by collectors. See the section on "Herpetology and the Law". Of course, a good conservation principle is always to collect no more animals than you have a real need for. Wholesale collecting and selling animals to pet or hide dealers is not a legitimate excuse for collecting large numbers of animals and is in some cases illegal.

Many reptiles live within a more or less definite area called a home range. Inside this area are logs, leaf litter, or other types of cover which constitute the animal's microhabitat. If collectors destroy this microhabitat, they may cause the loss of many unseen animals. Cover which has been turned in search of reptiles should be replaced when possible. It may take many years for natural processes to replace habitat and a devastated area is worthless for collecting, as well as being less suitable for its inhabitants.

COLLECTING EQUIPMENT

Most nonpoisonous snakes can be collected by hand, but a grasping device like a snake tong (available from Pilstrom Tong Company, Ft. Smith, Arkansas) can assist in the catch. Such a tool is very useful for capturing and handling poisonous specimens. Nooses are not recommended for use on snakes. Probably the most useful implement for general collecting is the potato rake. It can be used to move and lift objects, rake leaf litter and soil, and as a snake hook. The rake should be of heavy construction with thick, blade-like prongs. Those with round, wire-type prongs break too easily. A strong snake hook made from a golf putter, whip sickle, or piece of angle iron will also suffice. If sturdy enough, these can be used to move material and to pin a snake carefully to the ground until it can be maneuvered into a bag. Pinning snakes can cause them harm and extreme care should be taken if this method is used. An injured snake will not do well in captivity.

Capturing Reptiles

Reptiles can be transported in cloth bags made of muslin or similar materials that permit air to pass freely but are not too loosely woven. Pillow cases and cut off legs of denim jeans sewn shut at one end, both make good "herp" bags. Coarsely woven bags like gunnysacks are not suitable. Bags should not have worn places or even the smallest holes. Tops of the bags should be tied in an overhand knot —do not use string or ties to secure them.

Jars with screw lids used for home canning can be converted into containers for small animals. Screen wire or hardware cloth can be cut to replace the metal discs in the lid. Damp paper towels placed in the jar will protect the animals from desiccation and from being bumped around. Avoid putting bags or jars into direct sunlight or on the floor a a car that will be travelling a long distance. Heat can quickly kill reptiles. For the same reason, do not leave captured specimens in a closed car which is sitting in the sun. Bags and jars can be placed in a closed styrofoam or other type of ice chest. This will not only insulate the animals from rapid temperature changes, but can help prevent accidental crushing and other physical harm. Also, if a specimen escapes a bag or jar, it will still be captive in the cooler. Every herpetologist has at least one painful story about the prize that escaped in the car.

WHERE AND WHEN TO LOOK

Very few species are found in all habitats, so refer to the Florida habitat species charts and read the species accounts for those animals you are seeking before taking to the field. The time of year and time of day are important for many species. When it is too hot or cold, reptiles are not likely to be easily found. When the sun is strong and temperatures high, it is best to collect in the cooler hours of the morning or late afternoon as the sun is setting. The opposite is true when the weather is generally cool.

Despite efforts by local officials and conservationists, people still persist in dumping trash on the back roads of the state. Though unsightly, these trash piles, allowed to age a year or so, are ideal collecting sites for many reptiles, especially if sheet metal, boards, stoves or similar large, flat surfaced items of cover are among the refuse. The combination of cover and insects, rodents, and other food attract many species, including lizards, rat snakes, king snakes and rattlesnakes. Old abandoned houses with building materials scattered about also make excellent collecting sites. Be sure that the premises are abandoned before disturbing anything. The rights of property owners must always be respected.

Heavy-soled shoes and gloves should be worn when collecting in these areas to prevent injury from rusty nails, broken glass, and other sharp objects. A heavily constructed potato rake is ideal for lifting cover or tearing trash apart.

ROAD CRUISING

One of the most successful collecting techniques in Florida is night road cruising. However, just as with fishing, the wrong nights may yield nothing, even when conditions appear ideal. The weather conditions of the moment or even the previous day, the type of road surface, and the surrounding habitat are important things that may determine when and where to collect.

Road cruising is generally most successful from one hour before sunset to two or three hours after. Occasionally, pre-dawn and early morning hours are also productive. The best collecting occurs during moderate rains, or during initial sunny periods following an afternoon shower.

The best roads are secondary blacktops, although some dirt roads are highly productive. A few major highways may be good collecting areas, however the safety factor and the unlikelihood of collecting unharmed specimens make them less desirable.

Roadways through wetlands and pine flatwoods, or those which separate wet habitats from drier ones are usually good. Roads through open farmland, suburbs, or drastically modified habitat are usually poor for cruising. However, it is often difficult to predict what section of highway may produce good results.

Safety precautions must be taken when road cruising. Never stop directly on a well traveled highway; pull off onto the shoulder. Someone other than the driver should retrieve specimens. When safety allows, drive under 35 mph, with two observers scanning both sides of the road. Flashlights or headlamps are a must, but should never be directed toward oncoming traffic. Persons leaving the car should wear light-colored clothing and should not get so involved in the chase that they become unaware of traffic. No specimen is worth risking a life.

Make sure of the identity of your specimen before you pick it up. Under poor visibility conditions, some poisonous snakes may not be immediately recognizable. Some "look alike" species such as the southern hognose snake and pigmy rattlesnake, may appear even more alike at night. It would be better to let an unidentified snake escape than to make a dangerous misidentification. If you find an apparently dead poisonous snake, handle it as though it were alive; it may only be temporarily stunned and still capable of biting.

Do not carry firearms in your car and do not collect near occupied houses. Most people view a slow-moving vehicle on a back road at night with suspicion and may notify authorities. A gun in the car could lead you to be mistaken for a deer jacklighter, cattle rustler, or other law breaker.

FIELD NOTES

Valuable information can be obtained from field notes made on collecting trips and logs kept on specimens maintained in captivity. Many field collectors keep a loose-leaf notebook of standard size, while others use a pocket-sized or clipboard type. In any case, notes should be kept in chronological order. Specimens collected should be assigned a field number which is entered into the notes and also placed on the specimen tag, or feeding chart accompanying the animal. The data in the note book should be complete, concise, and include the following: date, locality (i.e. state, county, road or waterway, air distance from nearest post office or map coordinates), species collected in that locality, specimen field number, collector(s), type of habitat, microhabitat, and weather conditions.

Additional information such as routes traveled, distances, expenses, times, and other activities, and a summary of your observations may be valuable in the future. The information you omit may someday be the information you need.

PHOTOGRAPHY

Wildlife photography has become a major hobby in the United States, and many herpetologists have found it as enjoyable to photograph amphibians and reptiles in the wild as to collect them. Also, photographs of habitats and animal behavior taken on field trips may prove to be valuable.

Most reptiles are rather small and require close-up lenses and flash or strobe equipment for good results. Some are difficult to approach and telephoto lenses are required. It is often advantageous to capture the subject and pose it under the right lighting conditions. Many amphibians and reptiles will eventually tire and calm down long enough to be posed in the desired stance. Success in this endeavor requires considerable patience, but the rewards are well worth the time spent.

typical entry in field notes log

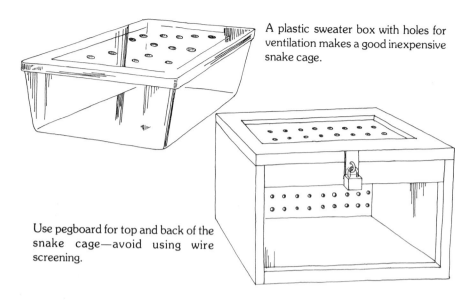

A plastic sweater box with holes for ventilation makes a good inexpensive snake cage.

Use pegboard for top and back of the snake cage—avoid using wire screening.

MAINTAINING REPTILES IN CAPTIVITY

Snakes should be maintained in a clean, dry, well-ventilated cage. The cage may consist of an aquarium with a tight-fitting screen or peg board top, a plastic shoe or sweater box that has holes drilled in the top and sides for smaller snakes, or a wooden, glass-fronted cage with peg board back and top. Screen should not be used. The bottom of the cage should be covered with newspaper or brown shipping paper that can be easily replaced when soiled. A small dish of fresh water should be provided in the cage at all times. A small box should be supplied to give the snake a dark retreat to hide in. Most snakes do well if fed once a week on the diet specified for each species in the account section. Details on maintaining snakes are available in numerous books; consult the bibliography section for recommended references.

Poisonous snakes should not be kept in captivity by the amateur herpetologist. The State of Florida has specific regulations about maintaining poisonous snakes, and a special permit is required.

PRESERVED COLLECTIONS

Many young herpetologists dislike the idea of killing and preserving a handsome reptile or amphibian which they have captured. Unfortunately, some of these same people are too often prone to allow valuable specimens to deteriorate, die, and be discarded once their novelty has worn off. While the days of wholesale collecting and pickling of amphibians and reptiles are hopefully gone, preserved collections, carefully made and curated for scientific purposes, can be an invaluable resource. Important specimens should be donated to a museum or other institution where collections are professionally maintained.

One excellent but often overlooked source of specimens for collections is animals found dead on the road (known as "DOR's" among herpetologists). If more unintentionally killed amphibians and reptiles had been preserved over the years, especially the rarer species, our knowledge of distribution, reproduction, and other aspects of their biology would be greater than it is today.

Complete information on preserving amphibians and reptiles is provided in "A Guide to the Preservation Techniques for Amphibians and Reptiles" by George Pisani which is available through the Society for the Study of Amphibians and Reptiles, Publications Secretary, Miami University, Oxford, Ohio 45056. Information may also be obtained by contacting the Department of Herpetology, Florida State Museum, University of Florida, Gainesville, Florida 32611, or by contacting the biology department at any university in your region.

Specimens can be stored in a cooler with ice, or in a freezer before preserving. If the specimens are to be frozen for some time, they should be placed in a plastic bag or other waterproof container and covered with water. Be sure that all collecting information is placed in the bag with the specimen.

SNAKE BITE

Statistics show that the potential danger of highway accidents is at least a hundred times greater than the chance of being bitten by a poisonous snake. Further, the odds of being killed by lightning are greater than being killed by a snake bite. Very few people are bitten by poisonous snakes in Florida each year and of these very few die. A large number of these bites probably occur when people accidentally come into contact with the snakes, usually by stepping on them. Others are bitten when trying to kill or snake or handling one that was assumed dead. Herpetologists and other collectors are by no means immune to poisonous snake bite, and every year a number are bitten either while collecting or by a "pet" poisonous snake. Preventing poisonous snake bite, like preventing any other accident, is a matter of common sense. Virtually every natural habitat in Florida supports at least one species of poisonous snake. If you are collecting reptiles, familiarize yourself with the poisonous species and leave them alone. It seems that nearly every snake collector eventually enters a stage where collecting and keeping poisonous snakes is the thing to do. This desire should be discouraged except for the most serious student. Leave the handling of the poisonous snakes up to professionals who have a definite purpose for keeping these dangerous animals.

Despite all the tall tales, there are no aggressive snakes in Florida. Most rely on their protective coloration and lie still until danger has passed. However, many will stand their ground if threatened. The cottonmouth will often coil and open its mouth into a gaping yawn, displaying its prominent white interior.

The diamondback rattlesnake will coil and generally rattle, as will the other rattlesnakes. However, not all individuals will rattle, and the sound produced by the pigmy's rattle is so faint it is difficult to hear. All will usually just turn and bite if stepped upon. Therefore, instead of running at the first sound of a rattle, stand perfectly still until the snake is located. If it is within a couple of feet, remain still. Most frightened snakes will retreat when possible. If you are out of striking distance, simply move away. Don't try to kill or catch the snake, since many people are bitten when trying to kill the snake they happened across.

FIRST AID

Many people fear that a poisonous snake bite is instantly fatal, but this is extremely rare. The seriousness of a bite depends on many variables including the species, size, and health of the snake, and the health, size, and age of the victim. The location of the bite and amount of venom released are also factors. Many poisonous snakes bite without releasing their venom, while others may deliver a large dose. Categorization of the severity of a bite is very important in treatment. The classes of snake bite are described in an article entitled, "Poisonous Snakebite: A Review" by Dr. L.H.S. Van Mierop, published in the Journal of the Florida Medical Association. These range from no envenomation, where only fang marks are present with little or no pain or swelling, to very severe, where the local reaction develops with severe swelling, blisters, and pain. These symptoms are for pit viper bites. In bites from coral snakes, there may be little or no swelling or pain and the symptoms may be delayed for many hours. Eventually, respiratory paralysis will set in, with possibly complete paralysis following.

First aid for snake bite again begins with common sense. There are many accounts of snake bites which were greatly complicated by an overzealous first aider. Avoid panic, and get the victim to a hospital as quickly as possible.

In Dr. Van Mierop's article, he lists the following steps for first aid to snake bite victims:

1. Keep the victim calm and reassured. Immobilize bitten area and, if possible, keep below the heart level.

2. Apply constricting band (not a tourniquet) about 1½ inches (4 cm) from the bite and between the bitten limb and the body. Tighten the band to just indent the skin. Release every 30 minutes for about one minute.

3. Wash or wipe clean the area around the fang marks.

4. If the bite was from a pit viper (identify the snake) and it begins to swell, a small ¼" (.64 cm) incision should be made across each fang mark. The cut should just go through the skin. Suction should be applied with a kit or by mouth. This treatment will be ineffective 30 minutes after the bite. This method of first aid is not effective for coral snake bites.

Such treatment is not necessary unless the snake was large or the bite severe. Do not waste time on first aid if a medical facility is within a reasonable distance.

A detailed description of medical treatment is outlined in the Van Mierop article (see literature section), which should prove helpful to a medical staff with little or no experience in treating snake bite.

Snake Bite

NONPOISONOUS BITES

The bites of most nonpoisonous snakes will leave a series of puncture wounds, usually in a horseshoe shape. Others, like the large watersnakes and the coachwhip, may produce a series of lacerations. These wounds should be throughly washed and treated with disinfectant. If the needle-like teeth are broken off in the wound, they should be removed to avoid infection.

NATURAL HISTORY

Very little is known about the origin of snakes, although it is accepted that they are derived from lizard-like creatures. Most of the fossil remains that have been found are vertebrae, the earliest ones dating from the lower Cretaceous, about 130 million years ago. The snake fossil record in Florida beginning with the Miocene contains numerous snakes, including a rattlesnake larger than the largest known diamondback.

CLASSIFICATION

Snakes, lizards, and the burrowing tropical group called amphisbaenians are grouped together in the order squamata because they all possess paired reproductive organs, the hemipenes of the male, and hatchlings have an egg tooth on their snout.

Very few characteristics separate snakes from lizards. Through parallel evolution some lizards such as the glass lizards have lost their legs probably adapting to their burrowing way of life. Most lizards, however, have legs, as well as external ear openings, small belly scales, and eyelids which distinguish them from snakes.

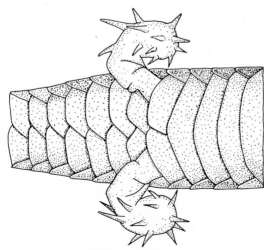

hemipenes of a male hognose snake

Snakes have no legs or internal skeletal structures to support them. The boas and pythons do have a vestigial pelvic bone to which are attached external hook-like spurs on either side of the anal plate. These are used in breeding and no longer aide in movement.

LOCOMOTION

Snakes exhibit two basic forms of movement—rectilinear locomotion or the caterpillar crawl, and serpentine motion. The caterpillar crawl results from a series of muscular movements from the head back toward the tail. The belly scales obtain traction in this way, causing the snake to move forward very slowly in a straight line. It is this type of movement that allows climbing snakes like the rat snakes to ascend the trunks of trees.

The more common form of locomotion in snakes is serpentine motion, in which the snake moves forward by pushing against objects with the sides of the belly scales and body causing the body to take a double-S position. A similar motion is used when a snake swims, as they all can.

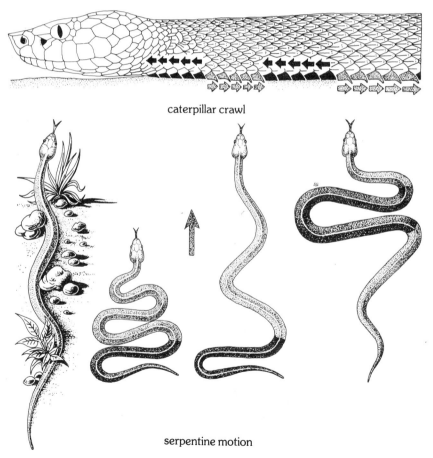

caterpillar crawl

serpentine motion

OBTAINING FOOD

All snakes are predators—they catch and kill other living animals. Their diet varies from species to species and in many cases is very selective.

Snakes locate their prey by using their keen sense of smell and by sight, particularly noting movement. There are three methods of catching and killing prey. The garter, water, indigo, and many of the smaller snakes catch their prey and hold it in their mouths with sharp, curved, needle-like teeth while swallowing it, usually while the victim is still alive. Other snakes like the rat snakes and kingsnakes are constrictors. After biting and holding the prey, they coil their bodies around the victim and squeeze until the animal is suffocated. Rarely is the animal actually crushed during the constriction. The third method of obtaining food is by poison. The elapids and crotalids have specialized teeth called fangs which are attached to ducts which lead to poison glands. It should be noted that the poison apparatus probably developed as a method of obtaining food and not for defense. The prey is bitten by the snake, and if small, is held in the snake's mouth until it dies. If the prey is large, it is bitten and then released. The poison may take some time to kill and the prey may move some distance. In that case the snake uses its sense of smell or its heat sensors to stalk its victim.

Snakes are noted for their ability to swallow objects several times larger than their head. This allows a wider variety of prey from which to select. Snakes can swallow very large prey because the bone structure of the skull is quite flexible, the jaws can unhinge and the skin between the scales is quite elastic. The snake uses its curved teeth and jaws to work the prey into the esophagus or the food tube. Wave-like constrictions then move the animal into the snake's stomach where digestion takes place.

Snakes feed periodically, depending on the availability of prey. The rate of digestion depends a great deal on temperature, size of prey, and on the size and age of the snake. After a good meal, some snakes may go several weeks or months without food; however, during warm months a snake may feed almost daily if prey is available.

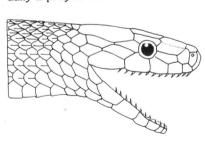

▲ rat snake—note sharp curved teeth for holding prey

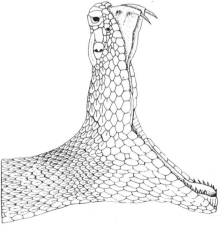

Rattlesnake fangs are hinged and ▶ become erect when the mouth is opened.

BEHAVIOR

We know very little about snakes in their natural habitat. We know very little about the size of their home ranges, how far they travel, their social interactions, the type of microhabitats used at different times of the year, or about most other aspects of their daily lives. Though we have learned a considerable amount from captive animals in zoos, museums, and private collections, the secretive nature of snakes in the wild makes observation very difficult.

In an effort to extend our knowledge of snakes in the wild, many herpetologists are studying snake behavior by marking them with small radioactive tags or radio transmitters. This allows the researcher to locate the animal at any time. These are crucial studies, particularly when endangered species are involved.

SENSES

Smell: All smells are actually caused by chemical particles in the air. A snake's flicking tongue picks up these particles from the air or from a scent trail on the ground. When the tongue is drawn into the mouth, its surface comes in contact with the sensory lining of the Jacobson's organ, chemical-sensitive tissue that is connected to the brain by a branch of the olfactory nerves. This method of smelling is quite well developed and replaces the usual method of smell found in most vertebrates.

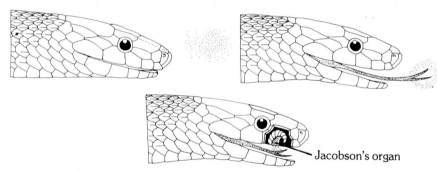

Jacobson's organ

sense of smell in snakes

Hearing: Snakes lack an external ear and ear drum. This affects their ability to hear airborne sounds, but they are by no means deaf. Vibrations, especially those from the substrate, are picked up through the body and particularly through the jaw bones.

Sight: Studies on some snakes have shown that they can see moving objects at more than 328 yards (300 m). Snakes have a wide field of vision but with little clarity. Only a few very specialized snakes—none of which are found in Florida—have binocular vision.

Touch and heat: Just like many other vertebrates, snakes have heat and touch sensors distributed evenly over their entire body surface. Because of the apparent hardness of their scales, we often overlook these senses, except when an obvious feature is present, as are the heat sensing pits of the crotalidae.

Natural History

REPRODUCTION

Snakes can be divided into two groups, those that bear live young and those that lay eggs. The species that bear live young actually maintain shell-less eggs, with yolk and egg membranes within the body. Generally the female does not provide nourishment to the developing embryo. When it is born, the young snake is coiled inside an opaque membrane which is quickly ruptured by the egg tooth and movements of the young snake.

JIM BRIDGES

Newborn hatching—note slits in egg caused by egg tooth.

JIM BRIDGES

Florida kingsnake laying eggs

Natural History

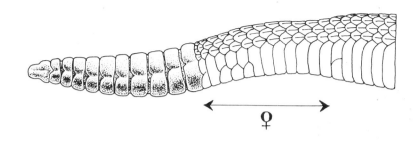

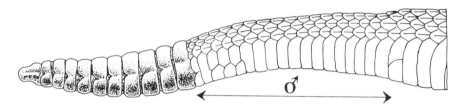

Males usually have proportionately longer tails than females. Tail length is measured from the cloaca or center of the anal plate.

The shells of externally laid snake eggs are leathery, most being oblong and whitish. Some are smooth while others are rough in texture, depending on the species. Snakes generally lay their eggs in rotting logs, soil or burrows where the humidity is high and the temperature usually warm. If the eggs are too cool or too warm, deformities and fatalities are increased. In captivity, eggs hatch normally if the temperature is kept around 80° F (26.6° C). Depending on the temperature, most snake eggs will hatch in 60 to 90 days.

Breeding season varies from one species to another. Males probably locate females by smell, seeking the pheromones released by the female. Once the female is located, the male will enter into courtship ritual with her. Again depending on the species, the male may rub his chin on the female's head and back or may even savagely bite the female's neck until breeding is complete. If the female is receptive, the male intertwines his tail around the female until the cloacas are in line. Then the male hemipenes is everted and inserted into the female's receptacle at the base of the cloaca. The sperm is then released. Snakes have been known to bear young several years after mating, indicating that sperm can be stored for a long time.

No parental care has been observed in any of the Florida snakes. The rainbow and mud snake females will attend the eggs but show not defense when nests are disturbed. Some pythons (an Old World family not found in Florida) incubate their eggs by raising their body temperatures and wrapping around their clutch, and show some defensive posture when nests are disturbed.

Hatchling snakes appear similar to their parents, though some have different markings (racers, coachwhips, and others). Soon after hatching the young go through their first molt, after which they begin to forage for food.

Natural History

TEMPERATURE REGULATION

Like all reptiles, snakes are considered to be "cold-blooded", a term that refers to the inability of their body to produce heat as the warm-blooded birds and mammals do. In reality, the term ectothermic is more accurate, meaning the temperature is externally regulated and the blood temperature may, depending on the external environmental conditions, be quite warm. Most snakes cannot control their body temperature internally so temperature is regulated by movement within the environment, e.g. when a snake basks in the sun. Snakes can live within a temperature range from 39° to 98°F (4°-37°C). Each species has an optimal temperature where digestion and all other body processes function properly. This optimal temperature is reached by moving into warm areas such as sunny spots, or by retreating undercover or into water when the temperature becomes too high.

In the winter when temperatures get too low for a snake's body processes to function properly, it will go under cover, often underground, usually where the temperature does not go below 39°F (4°C) and the snake will become dormant. This state is referred to as hibernation, but in Florida a true state of hibernation or dormancy is not reached except in the northernmost counties.

Temperature requirements are often ignored by people who wish to keep snakes as pets. Brown snakes, redbelly snakes and a few others with apparently low optimal temperatures will do well in a cage without a heat source which is in an air conditioned house with a temperature around 68° F (20° C). Most snakes, however, need an area in the cage where the temperature is 86° F (30° C). This may be accomplished by using a light bulb over or a heating pad under one end of the cage as a heat source. The snake can then choose the area when its body temperature needs raising as it would in the wild by basking, or it can find a cooler spot away from the heat source. (Refrain from putting snake cages in the sun since the temperature of the entire cage may become too high and kill the captive.

SHEDDING

Like most animals, snakes shed their skin. This allows for growth and the replacement of worn out skin and scales. Snakes may shed once or many times a year, depending on growth rate, age, and the general health of the individual. As a snake prepares to shed, the eyes and general color become pale or cloudy due to the secretion of a milky fluid between the old and the new skin layers. This condition is referred to as "opaque" or "premolt". During this time sight is impaired and the snake is often irritable. Snakes often go under cover at this time, since they are more vulnerable due to impaired vision. After several days the opaqueness clears and the snake begins to rub its head and neck against objects until the old skin catches and is pulled off, usually in one piece and inside out. Occasionally the skin will come off in pieces, especially in captivity where the relative humidity may be too low.

Old skin is usually shed in one piece and inside-out.

SNAKE DEFENSES

The primary defense of all snakes is their coloration and ability, even if brightly colored like the coral snake or scarlet kingsnake, to "disappear" into their habitat. Most snakes have camouflage coloration that permits them to effectively blend into the substrata of their environment. In addition, most snakes "freeze" when first alarmed, counting on their coloration to protect them. Most of their natural enemies such as the hawk, owl or raccoon have keen eyes and are attuned to movement. Therefore a snake at rest will usually remain that way; if it is already in motion when disturbed it will usually continue moving to more protective cover, assuming that it has already been seen. Some snakes may instantly turn and bite if touched or stepped on, though others will flee. Certain snakes have "threat" displays. The hognose will flatten its neck cobra-style and hiss loudly; this failing, it will feign death by rolling over on its back, often with mouth agape and tongue hanging out. Many snakes will flatten their heads and bodies, apparently, to look more ominous. The cottonmouth will gape its jaws displaying its cottony white mouth and extended fangs. Of course the rattlesnake will often, but not always, rattle its tail when alarmed. In fact many, if not most, snakes will rattle their tails when disturbed. When this occurs in dry leaves, the listener will often feel certain they heard a rattlesnake instead of the harmless rat snake actually there. Some snakes like the coral and ringneck will coil their tails in an attempt to confuse a predator so it will not know which end truly is the head.

Poison should be considered a method of obtaining food rather than a main method of defense. No studies have shown how effective poison is against natural snake enemies such as hawks, raccoons, herons or alligators. It probably isn't very effective, but poison has been shown to be an efficient means of obtaining food.

CHECKLIST OF FLORIDA SNAKES AND THEIR HABITATS

The following checklists are designed to give the reader an idea of the habitats that are used by each species of snake in Florida and their relative abundance (C = common, U = uncommon, R = rare) in that habitat.

The chart should be used with the distribution maps, species accounts, and habitat descriptions. For example, by checking the map and account of the short-tailed snake, one will see that this species is only found in central Florida counties and is restricted to very dry, sandy habitats.

One should note that just because a species is not listed in a particular habitat does not necessarily mean that it may not occur there, the reverse also being true. However, the listings are based on the most likely habitats used and the probability of locating the species in that habitat. Page number of account is in parentheses after the species name.

SNAKES

	Pine Flatwoods	Sand Pine-Rosemary Scrub	Longleaf Pine-Turkey Oak	Xeric Oak Hammock	Mesic Hammock	Hydric Hammock	Tropical Hammock
Brown Snake							
Florida (132)	C				C	U	
Marsh (134)					C	U	
Midland (134)					C		
Coachwhip, Eastern (97)	U	C	C	U			
☠ Copperhead, Southern (155)			C	R			
☠ Coral Snake, Eastern (152)	U	C	C	U	U		U
☠ Cottonmouth, Florida (158)	C				U	U	
Crayfish Snake							
Glossy (122)	R					R	
Gulf (124)	R					R	
Striped (120)						R	
Crowned Snake							
Coastal Dunes (141)		U					
Florida (141)	R	C	C	C			C
Peninsula (139)	C	U	U	R	R		
Rim Rock (141)	R	R					R
Southeastern (137)	R	U	C	U			
Earth Snake							
Rough (148)	R		R	R			
Smooth (150)	R			R	R		
Garter Snake							
Bluestripe (148)						U	
Eastern (146)	U				U	U	R
Green Snake, Rough (116)	C		U	U	C	U	C
Hognose							
Eastern (81)	C	U	C	U	C		
Southern (85)	U	C	C	U			
Indigo Snake, Eastern (65)	U	U	U	U	R	U	R
Kingsnake, Common (90)							
Eastern (92)	U				C	U	
Florida (92)	U	R		U	R	U	U
Scarlet (94)	U	R	U	R	U		U
Mole Kingsnake (87)	R		U				
Mud Snake, Eastern (76)					R	U	
Pine Snake, Florida (118)	R	U	U				
Pine Woods Snake (126)	U	U	U		U		
Queen Snake (124)							
Racer							
Brownchin (62)	U		U	U			
Everglades (62)			U	C		C	C
Southern Black (59)	C	U	C	U	C	C	

Terrestrial Habitats

Table — habitat occurrence matrix (C = Common, U = Uncommon, R = Rare)

Temperate Deciduous Forest	Farmlands, Fields and Disturbed Areas	Human Habitations, Golf Courses and Trash Piles	Coastal Beaches and Dunes	Salt Marsh	Mangrove Swamp	Freshwater Marsh	Temporary Ponds and Roadside Ditches	Permanent Ponds and Lakes	Cypress Swamps and Domes	Gum Swamps and River Swamps	Rivers	Small Streams and Creeks	Canals
C	C	C							U	U			
C	C	C							C	C			
	U	U	U										
U	R	U											
R	R	U											
				R	R	C	C	C	C	C	C	C	R
							R	R	U	U	U		
							R	R	U	U	U		
						C		C	C	C	U		
U		U	U										
R		U											
		U											
R		U											
	R	U				U	C	C	C		C	C	R
	U	U					C	C	U				R
R	U	U	R										
	U	R											
	U	U					C	U	U		R		
R	R	U	U			U	U	U			U	U	U
R	R												
						C	U	C	C	C	C	C	
	R	R	R										
	R	U											
R											R	R	
	U	U	U			R	U	U					
U	C	C	R				U	U					

Aquatic Habitats

49

SNAKES

	Pine Flatwoods	Sand Pine-Rosemary Scrub	Longleaf Pine-Turkey Oak	Xeric Oak Hammock	Mesic Hammock	Hydric Hammock	Tropical Hammock
Rainbow Snake							
Rainbow (79)						R	
South Florida (81)						R	
Rat Snake							
Corn (67)	C	U	C	U	U	U	U
Everglades (71)					U		C
Gray (71)	C		U	C	U	U	
Yellow (70)	C	U	U	C	C	U	
Rattlesnake							
Dusky Pigmy (165)	C	C	C	U			
Eastern Diamondback (161)	C	C	C	R	R		R
Timber (163)	C				U	R	
Redbelly Snake							
Florida (134)	U				U		
Northern (135)	U				U		
Ribbon Snake							
Bluestripe (143)							
Eastern (143)				U	C		
Peninsula (143)					U		R
Ringneck Snake							
Key (64)	U						
Southern (62)	C	R	R	U	U		U
Salt Marsh Snake							
Atlantic (110)							
Gulf (110)							
Mangrove (110)							
Scarlet Snake							
Florida (57)	C	R	U	U	U		
Northern (59)	C			U	U		
Short-tailed Snake (130)		R	R	R			
Swamp Snake							
North Florida (128)	U					R	
South Florida (130)	R					R	R
Water Snake							
Banded (110)	U						
Brown (112)						C	
Florida (106)						U	
Florida Green (100)						C	
Midland (114)						U	U
Redbelly (103)						R	
Yellowbelly (104)						R	

Terrestrial Habitats

Temperate Deciduous Forest	Farmlands, Fields and Disturbed Areas	Human Habitations, Golf Courses and Trash Piles	Coastal Beaches and Dunes	Salt Marsh	Mangrove Swamp	Freshwater Marsh	Temporary Ponds and Roadside Ditches	Permanent Ponds and Lakes	Cypress Swamps and Domes	Gum Swamps and River Swamps	Rivers	Small Streams and Creeks	Canals
										R	R	U	R
											R	U	
U	C	C			R				U	U			
U	C	C	U		U			U	U	U			
	U	U				U		U	U				
	U	U	R	U		C		U	U				
U										R			
				U			C	U	C	C	U	C	
	U	U				C	C	U	C	C	U	C	R
	U	U				C	U	U	C	C		C	
C	U	R							C				
		C											
		R		R	R								
		R		U	U				C				
R		R							C				
	R												
						C	C	C	C	C		C	
						C	C	C	C	C		C	R
						C	C	C	C	C	C	C	U
						U	R	C	U	U	C	U	U
						C	C	C	C	C	C	U	C
						U	R	C	U	U	C	U	
						U		U	U		U	U	
									U		U	U	

51

Aquatic Habitats

THE SNAKES

FAMILY COLUBRIDAE

More than two thirds of the 3,000 living species of snakes are in the family colubridae. They are the most common group of snakes on all continents except Australia.

In this large family there is tremendous diversity, even among the Florida snakes. Members are as diverse as the giant indigos and the tiny crowned snake, the pudgy hognose and the arboreal green snake. The species in this family that are found in Florida are not considered poisonous to man (some may have saliva toxic to other animals), but there are some poisonous species in this family in other parts of the world.

There are several characteristics that members of this vast group have in common. None have the remnants of the pelvic girdle or spurs reminicent of hind legs as found in the primitive boas and pythons. Most have lost the left lung while in others it is greatly reduced. All have common developments in skull and jaw structure and all have solid teeth (unlike the viperids and elapids).

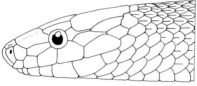

Non-poisonous snake can be distinguished by round pupils. All colubrids in Florida have round pupils. But, the coral snakes, the New World elapids, which also have round pupils, are poisonous.

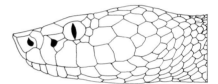

The poisonous viperids have vertical (elliptical) pupils and heat sensing pits.

FAMILY ELAPIDAE

This is primarily an Old World family, found chiefly in Australia where most snakes are members, and in Asia and Africa where cobras, mambas and kraits are the most notorious family representatives. The sea snakes of the Pacific and Indian oceans are members of this group. In the New World, the elapids are represented by the coral snakes, two of which are found in the United States.

In many ways, the elapids resemble the colubrids. They have rounded pupils, narrow snouts (as opposed to the viperids) and generally do not fit the "rules" of being poisonous snakes. The elapids have straight, hollow fangs located in front of the upper jaw, which are attached to an enclosed venom canal.

Many people believe that these docile snakes must chew to inject their venom. This may not be the case and any bite from a coral snake should be treated as dangerous. They rarely strike like other snakes, even when stepped on. Other misinformation is that the bite of a coral snake kills in seconds and is always fatal. In fact, it may require many hours before symptoms appear and there is antivenin available (see snake bite section).

There is considerable controversy about whether or not the scarlet kingsnake and the scarlet snake are mimics of the coral. It is a hypothesis that is very difficult to prove. However, the brightly banded snakes do display warning colors and patterns that may be recognized by some predators, and thus avoided.

FAMILY VIPERIDAE, SUB-FAMILY CROTALIDAE

The snakes in this group are distinguished by their hollow, hinged fangs located in the front of the mouth.

Pit vipers or crotalidae are found in the New World and Asia. They are so named because of the facial pit which is found below and between the eye and nostril on either side of the head. This pit is made up of two chambers and is highly sensitive to infrared radiation (heat), and thus can serve as a direction finder in locating warm blooded prey or predators. This well-developed sense can detect temperatures differences of less than 0.22°C and can even be used to follow the "heat" trail left behind by a mammal.

Unique to the New World are the rattlesnakes, members of the crotalidae which have modified tails, the rattle. The rattle is made of keratin, a substance similar to the human fingernail. Each time the rattlesnake sheds, a new loosely interlocking segment is added to the tail. When moved, the segments vibrate against each other producing the familiar warning buzz.

The age of a rattlesnake cannot be determined by the size or number of segments in the rattle. Depending on growth rate and shedding, a snake may add several segments to the rattle each year. Also, the rattle is often broken off after a couple of years and an adult rattlesnake that has the original button at the end of its rattle is uncommon.

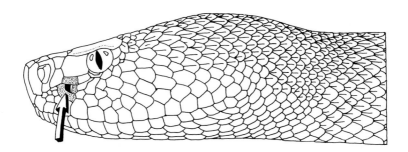

Crotalidae, or pit vipers, are named for the heat sensing pit found on each side of the head.

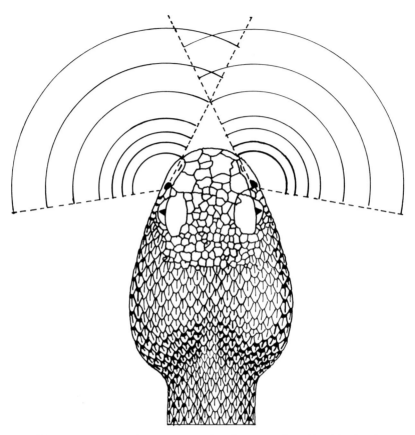

Heat waves vex into heat sensitive chambers on either side of the head.

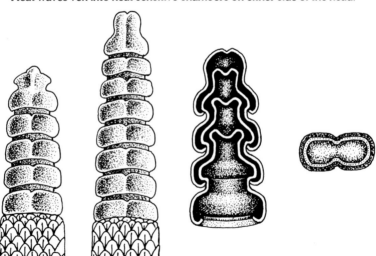

no button—
broken rattle

rattle ending
in button

rattle bi-section

rattle cross section

The Snakes

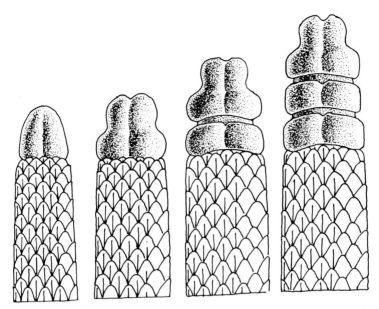

Rattle growth—a loosely fitting segment is added to the tail each time the snake sheds.

INTERPRETING THE SPECIES ACCOUNTS

For those not familiar with some of the terminology, it may be necessary to refer to the glossary or to the labeled illustrations. The first, italicized name listed at the top of each species account is, of course, the scientific name. Scientific names are necessary to provide continuity. While a snake may be called by many common names, and often two or three different snakes may have the same common name, a snake is given one specific latinized scientific name. This name always belongs to only one species of snake. The first name is called the *genus*. Many snakes may have the same genus name. This means that they are all grouped together and believed to be related. Each snake also has a second name in the scientific name called the *species*. Another name may follow the species. This is generally refered to as *subspecies*.

The species name is given to generally one specific kind of snake. If there are other snakes that a much alike but with only minor differences in color or form and are separated in their ranges, they may be given a subspecies name. They will all share a common genus name and species name, but the subspecies name will be different.

The Snakes

Scientific Names	Common Names
Nerodia taxispilota	brown water snake
Nerodia fasciata pictiventris	Florida water snake
Nerodia fasciata clarki	Gulf salt marsh snake
Nerodia fasciata taeniata	Atlantic salt marsh snake

These all share the genus name *Nerodia*. The brown water snake, *Nerodia taxispilota*, has a different species name than the Florida water snake, Gulf salt marsh snake, and Atlantic salt marsh snake, which share the genus and species names, *Nerodia fasciata*, but the subspecies names are all different, designating each as separate from the others. Note that some subspecies are important or different enough to warrant an entire account while others are mentioned briefly within an account under the heading **Subspecies**. Any scientific name of three parts indicates that it represents a subspecies and that other subspecies, though not necessarily found in Florida, must be found somewhere. In some accounts the heading **Color Variants** is used. This is to indicate populations that vary considerably from the description given for the species. At one time many of these were considered subspecies.

A point of confusion may be the names between the scientific name and the common name. This is the name(s) of the person who first used that scientific name. For example: *Coluber constrictor priapus* Dunn and Wood **Southern Black Racer**. The authors of this scientific name are Dunn and Wood. Sometimes the animal is moved to a genus other than the one in which it was originally classified. In this case, the name of the author of the original species name is placed in parentheses. For example: *Thamnophis sauritus sauritus* (Linnaeus) **Eastern Ribbon Snake**. Linnaeus originally named this snake. He called it *Coluber saurita* in 1766. Since then this snake has had nearly a dozen various scientific names. It was called *Thamnophis sauritus sauritus* by Ruthven in 1908. Since its name is now different from the original given it by Linnaeus in 1766, Linnaeus' name is now placed in parentheses.

POISONOUS SPECIES ARE DISTINGUISHED BY THE SYMBOL ☠ .

ABOUT THE MAPS

The county dots represent specimen records from that county. To be considered, specimens had to be preserved in a museum collection. Live specimens or preserved specimens in private collections were not considered because these are not usually available for study and the loss of them through time is more likely. Collections included in this survey included: The Florida State Museum, Carnegie Museum, U.S. Museum of Natural History, North Carolina State Museum, Tall Timbers Research Station, Florida Technological University, Auburn University, University of Michigan, American Museum of Natural History, California Academy of Science, Los Angeles County Museum, University of Kansas Museum of Natural History, Indiana University, Northwestern State University of Louisiana, University of Illinois, Tulane University, The Charleston Museum, and The Cleveland Museum. Locality data has been updated through 1988.

The Snakes

Counties without dots do not have specimens represented in the above collections. Dots with question marks indicate that the specimen and record is questionable.

Shaded areas approximate the range of the species, subspecies, or color variation. In all cases these are approximate and have never fully been determined.

Dots are centered in each county and do not represent exact localities. The decision to use the county dot method was based on the fact that most habitats are scattered islands in most cases and are not contiguous. Instead of trying to locate a specific locality, look for the proper habitat of a species within its range. A serious researcher will want to locate exact locality data available in the geographic files of research museums.

If a collector locates a specimen from a county not represented, he or she may want to notify a local museum or professional herpetologist in the above mentioned institutions. If the specimen has good accompanying data, it may be included in the collection.

SPECIES ACCOUNTS

Cemophora coccinea coccinea (Blumenbach)
Florida Scarlet Snake

Description: This coral snake mimic is a medium-sized snake reaching a maximum length of 31 inches (80 cm). Its back is saddled with red blotches which are encircled by black. The color between the blotches is yellowish to smoky gray. The light-colored scales are usually tipped with black. The head is small and the snout is pointed. *The belly is glossy white.*

RAY E. ASHTON, JR.

Florida scarlet snake

The Snakes—Colubrids

Similar Species: The coral snake and the scarlet kingsnake have bands that extend around the body.

Natural History: This colorful burrower inhabits upland, sandy-soiled habitats, and is most common in pine flatwoods. Rarely seen during the day, most scarlet snakes are seen crossing roads in the early evening and at night, but

Range of the Florida Scarlet Snake in Florida is designated by the open area, Northern Scarlet Snake by the ⁞⁞⁞ area. Insert map shows general distribution of *Cemophora coccinea* in the United States.

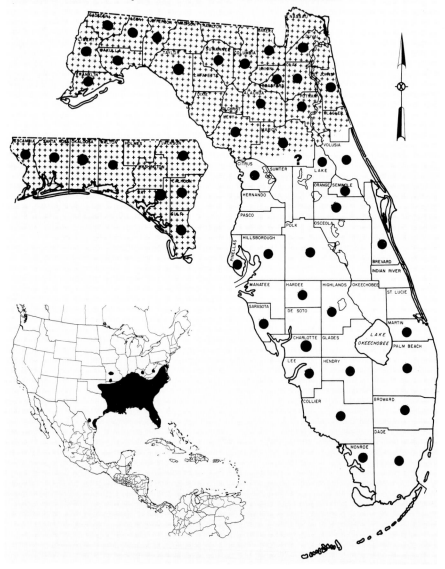

The Snakes—Colubrids

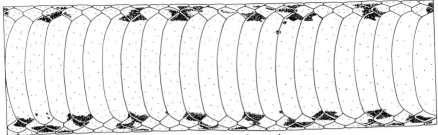
belly pattern—scarlet snake

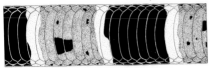
belly pattern—coral snake

belly pattern—scarlet kingsnake

specimens are occasionally collected under logs or in stumps. Small lizards and rodents and reptile eggs constitute the principal food of this constrictor. This docile snake doesn't do well in captivity, usually refusing food. Some success can be had if the snake is given loose sand to burrow in. Captive specimens may be induced to eat small live mice and skinks, which should be introduced, and the cage then covered during feeding.

Reproduction: Three to eight long white eggs are laid, probably under-ground. No natural nests have been recorded. Recently captured females have laid eggs in early July.

Subspecies:
Cemophora coccinea copei Jan **Northern Scarlet Snake** This sub-species occurs in the panhandle and the northern counties of the peninsula. It is very difficult to distinguish from the Florida race. The scales on the upper lip are six in this subspecies and the first black band touches the parietal scales.

Coluber constrictor priapus Dunn and Wood
Southern Black Racer

Description: Adults are a satiny black or slate gray and reach a maximum length of 70 inches (178 cm). The scales are large and smooth. The eye is large and has a rich brown iris. Chin and throat are usually white; nose may be brownish. The underside is slate gray to blue gray.

Juveniles: The young are totally different from the adults and resemble young coachwhips. They are slate gray in color with a row of large reddish tan spots down the back and smaller spots on the sides. Young coachwhips have dark wavy crosslines across the body.) The belly is whitish to gray with dark spots.

Similar Species: Indigos are stocky with a reddish or blackish chin. Coachwhips are usually whitish to tan toward the tail.

Natural History: The racer is one of the most common larger snakes found throughout Florida. It inhabits nearly all environments, but is found most

The Snakes—Colubrids   59

JOHN C. MURPHY

ED CASSANO

juvenile southern black racer

adult southern black racer

ROBERT S. SIMMONS

Everglades racer

The Snakes—Colubrids

commonly in brush covered, cutover areas near water. Unlike most snakes, the racer is a diurnal hunter, feeding on frogs, rodents, birds, lizards, and occasionally other snakes. The juveniles will eat insects. When hunting, a racer will sometimes crawl across open areas with its head raised off the ground, looking about alertly. When cornered, this snake will vibrate its tail and bite savagely. Usually

Range of the Southern Black Racer in Florida is designated by the open area, Brownchin Racer by the ⋮⋮⋮ area, Everglades Racer by the ▨ area. Insert map shows general distribution of *Coluber constrictor* in the United States.

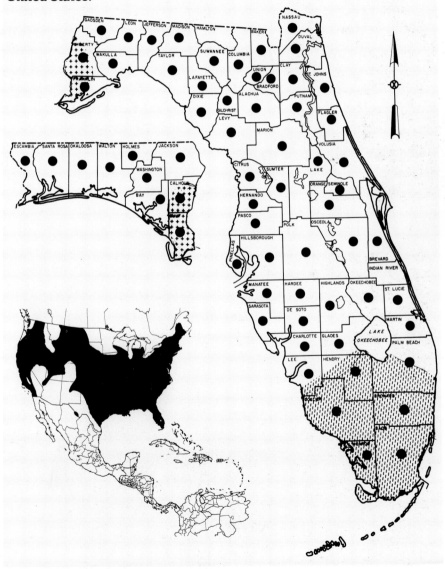

this behavior will continue in captivity. Its name "racer" indicates it is a fast moving snake; in fact some believe it can outrun a human. This is not true; however, the snake may be able to keep up a fast pace for a short distance.

Reproduction: Breeding occurs in early spring. Seven to 22 eggs are deposited in rotting stumps, logs, and old sawdust piles from midspring into the summer. The eggs are oval, white and have a rough surface. Hatching occurs in about 60 days.

Subspecies:

Coluber constrictor helvigularis Auffenberg **Brownchin Racer** This snake is like the black racer in size and shape, but the chin and lips are a light tan to chocolate brown.

Coluber constrictor paludicola Auffenberg and Babbitt **Everglades Racer** This racer is much lighter than other subspecies in overall coloration. It is gray blue to blue green above; the belly is white to light gray. The iris of the eye is usually brick red.

Diadophis punctatus punctatus (Linnaeus)
Southern Ringneck Snake

Description: This slender snake, reaching a maximum length of 18.5 inches (47 cm), is slate gray above with a broken orange-yellow ring around the neck. The small head is gray to gray black. The belly is bright yellow and changing to orange on the underside of the tail. *There is a row of black half moons down the center of the belly.*

Juveniles: Similar to adults.

Similar Species: Redbelly snakes have stripes on the back and lack the half moons on the belly.

Natural History: This attractive snake is found in moist open habitats such as those found near cypress heads in pine flatwoods. It lives in leaf litter and under logs. The ringneck feeds on ground skinks, earthworms, small salamanders—particularly the dwarf salamander, and other small animals that live in the moist leaf litter and sphagnum. It is most commonly found in the spring, and it becomes very difficult to find as summer approaches.

When alarmed, the ringneck thrashes around and coils its brightly colored tail, apparently trying to distract attention from its vulnerable head. It also expels a tremendous quantity of musk for such a small snake. They are common food of

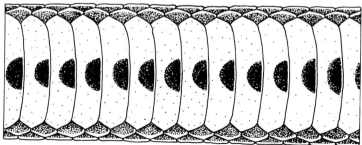

belly pattern—southern ringneck snake

the coral snake. The ringneck rarely attempts to bite, and even the largest specimen has a mouth and teeth too small to inflict a wound. Recent studies have shown that the ringneck may have toxic saliva.

Ringnecks are often found in groups of two or more, especially during hibernation. They do not do well in captivity, refusing to eat, although some individuals can be encouraged to eat small salamanders.

Range of the Southern Ringneck Snake in Florida is designated by the open area; Key Ringneck Snake in lower keys, below the line. Insert map shows general distribution of *Diadophis punctatus* **in the United States.**

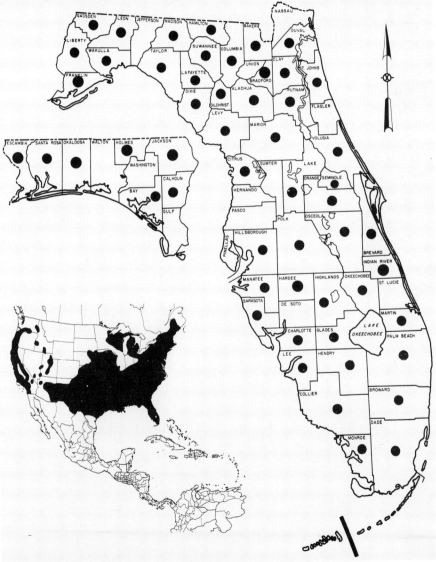

Reproduction: Four to seven narrow white eggs are laid in midsummer in rotting logs, stumps, or under leaf litter. Eggs hatch in 38-50 days.

Subspecies: *Diadophis punctatus acricus* Paulson **Key Ringneck Snake** This snake is known only from Big Pine Key, where it lives in pine habitat. It lacks a neck ring and has a pale gray head. This race is considered threatened due to loss of habitat.

R.W. VAN DEVENDER

southern ringneck snake

JIM BRIDGES

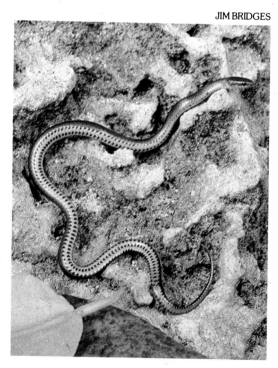

key ringneck snake

The Snakes—Colubrids

Drymarchon corais couperi   (Holbrook)
Eastern Indigo Snake

Description: This handsome serpent is the largest nonpoisonous snake in North America, reaching a length of 104 inches (263 cm). It is glossy blue black with smooth iridescent scales. The chin and throat may be rusty to blood red. Some individuals have white-blotched throats.

Range of the Eastern Indigo Snake in Florida. Insert map shows the general distribution of the species in the United States.

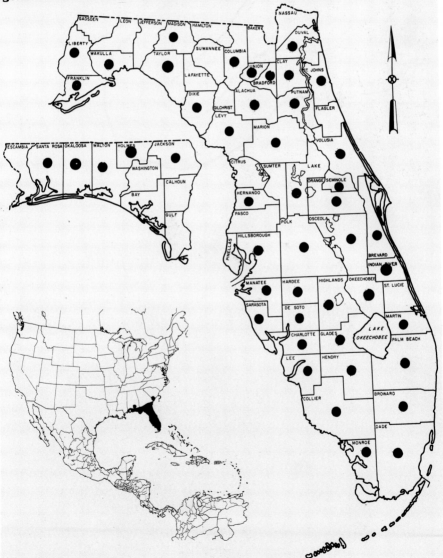

adult eastern indigo snake

juvenile eastern indigo snake

　　　　　　　　　　　　　　　　　　The Snakes—Colubrids

Juveniles: The young are usually similar to the adults, but some may be lighter and show a blotched dorsal pattern.

Similar Species: The black racer has a white or brown throat, and is much lighter in build.

Natural History: This snake is now considered by many to be threatened throughout its range. It has reached this status because of habitat destruction combined with extensive collecting pressures for the pet trade. In south Florida, the indigo seems to still be quite common in some areas. In much of its Florida range, this snake uses gopher tortoise burrows for shelter. The collecting of tortoise for food and gassing of burrows to collect rattlesnakes have also adversely affected this species. Indigos inhabit dry habitats that are bordered by water.

The indigo snake feeds on a variety of animals including reptiles, amphibians, small mammals, and birds. It appears especially fond of rat snakes. This snake catches its prey in powerful jaws similar to the method used by garter snakes. Despite its large size, the indigo does not kill its prey by constriction.

Special permits are required to keep this species in captivity.

Reproduction: Very little is known about reproduction in the wild, however, many people have successfully bred this species in captivity. Captive breeding takes place in late fall or early winter. Up to 11 large white eggs may be deposited during May or June. Where eggs are laid in the wild still remains a mystery. However, some reports have stated that eggs are laid in gopher *(Geomys)* burrows. The eggs hatch in about 90 days.

Elaphe guttata guttata (Linnaeus)
Corn Snake, Red Rat Snake

Description: This beautiful, medium-sized snake may reach a length of 72 inches (183 cm). It varies greatly in color but usually has a row of large red or rusty blotches with dark margins down the center of the back, and smaller ones on the sides. The background color may be gray, tan, yellowish or light orange. *The underside is a checkerboard of black and white squares.* Some individuals found in west-central Florida have gray dorsal blotches. The scales are weakly keeled.

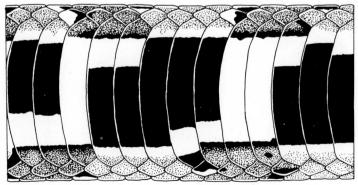

belly pattern—corn snake (red rat snake)

typical corn snake (red rat snake)

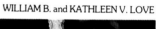

rare gray color phase corn snake (rat snake)

The Snakes—Colubrids

Juveniles: Similar to adults but with a grayer background color.

Similar Species: Some reddish, yellow rat snakes show blotches but also have stripes.

Natural History: This common snake is found in nearly all habitats and is often seen around old buildings and under trash piles. It feeds on birds and small mammals, particularly mice. Many farmers allow this beneficial species to

Range of the Corn Snake in Florida. Insert map shows general distribution of *Elaphe guttata* **in the United States.**

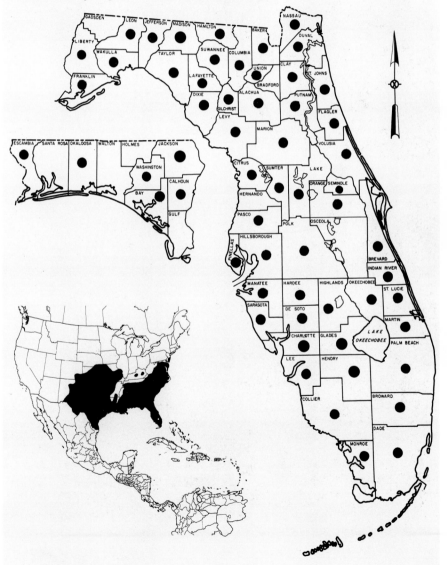

RAY E. ASHTON, JR.

Keys color variant—rosy rat snake

remain, while killing other snakes. When confronted, the corn snake will coil in an S-shape, vibrate its tail, and often bite savagely. After a short time in captivity, it tames nicely and does well on a mouse diet.

Reproduction: Breeding probably occurs in winter through spring. Up to 30 elongated white eggs are laid per clutch in late spring and early summer. Little is known about the natural nesting of this species. However, the author uncovered two clutches of eggs at the edge of an abandoned sawdust pile.

Color Variant: Rosy Rat Snake Found only in the lower keys, this population, considered by some as a subspecies, is different from the corn snake in that the blotches on the back are rarely marked with black. The belly is lightly marked with black if black markings are present at all. This population is considered threatened due to habitat destruction.

Elaphe obsoleta quadrivittata (Holbrook)
Yellow Rat Snake, Chicken Snake

Description: This large, attractive snake, which reaches a size of 84 inches (213 cm), usually is bright yellow to olive with four brown lateral—2 lateral, 2 dorsolateral—stripes. Some individuals may have faint blotches across the back. The head is yellowish brown to tan. The chin is white and the belly is light yellow to cream colored. The scales are weakly keeled.

Juveniles: The young may be blotched with light brown and appear more like a gray rat snake. The four dorsal stripes of adults are very faint in the juveniles.

Similar Species: Garter snakes and ribbon snakes have strongly keeled scales, and no more than three lateral stripes.

The Snakes—Colubrids

yellow rat snake (chicken snake)

Natural History: This snake is common along the edges of woodland habitats. It is often found in old buildings, barns, and trash piles. Occasionally it may be found in chicken coops, thus the yellow rat snake is often called the chicken snake. A highly arboreal snake, the yellow rat feeds on birds and their eggs as well as on small rodents. Like other rat snakes, it is a powerful constrictor, wrapping and suffocating its prey in strong coils. The edges of the belly plates are squared off and aid in climbing.

When alarmed, a yellow rat will coil with the upper half of the body in an S-shaped striking pose and will strike rapidly while vibrating its tail. Like other members of this group, this rat snake will release a strong but not unpleasant musk. Some predators like bobcats are often affected by the musk much like they are by catnip—they ignore the snake and roll around on the musk left by the yellow rat snake.

Rat snakes tame easily and if provided with a supply of live mice and chicks, will survive numerous years in captivity.

Reproduction: Four to 28 oblong, smooth eggs per clutch are usually laid during summer. The eggs have been found in rotting logs and railroad ties still buried in the ground. Breeding occurs in the spring.

Subspecies:

Elaphe obsoleta rossalleni Neill **Everglades Rat Snake** This questionable subspecies is bright orange above and below and has four distinct dark brown stripes, and a red tongue. This race is found in the Everglades of south Florida.

Elaphe obsoleta spiloides (Dumeril, Bibron, and Dumeril) **Gray Rat Snake, Oak Snake** **Description:** This large, often beautiful snake, reaching a length of 84 inches (213 cm), varies greatly in color. Some populations

The Snakes—Colubrids   71

Everglades rat snake

are a smoky-white gray with gray blotches surrounded by thin black lines. Others may be dark gray with brownish gray blotches. The head is uniformly gray to brownish. The scales are weakly keeled. The belly is gray with faint blotching. Some adults are striped. *Juveniles:* Similar to adults. *Similar Species:* Yellow rat snake juveniles are difficult to distinguish from gray rat snakes which have an overall gray blotched pattern. *Natural History:* The gray rat snake is commonly found in wooded areas around swamps, other wetlands, or open grasslands. Often they are found in old buildings and barns, even in suburbs and towns. An excellent climber, this race eats birds and their eggs. They also eat small rodents, which leads many farmers to spare this snake while killing most others. Like other rat snakes, the gray rat snake is a powerful constrictor. When alarmed, it will coil and strike repeatedly. After some handling, the gray rat snake tames nicely. It will do well in captivity if given live mice or chicks for food.

Color Variants:

Gulf Hammock Rat Snake   Some rat snakes in the Gulf hammock region have the blotched pattern coloration of gray rat snakes but also have distinct stripes like those found in yellow rat snakes. Similar patterns are found in other areas where the two subspecies meet.

Key Rat Snake   The lateral stripes are usually gray or gray brown. The back is tan to orange and is blotched like juvenile rat snakes.

juvenile gray rat snake

adult gray rat snake

The Snakes—Colubrids

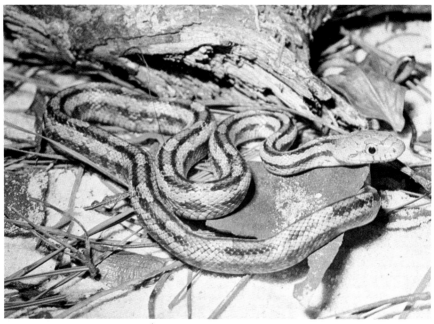

Gulf hammock color variant

key rat snake—color variant

The Snakes—Colubrids

Approximate range of the Yellow Rat Snake in Florida is designated by the open area, Gray Rat Snake by the ⣿ area, and the Everglades Rat Snake by the ⣿ area. The color forms (not recognized subspecies) known as the Gulf Hammock Rat Snake by the ⁘ area, the Key Rat Snake by the ‖‖ area. The insert map shows general distribution of *Elaphe obsoleta* in the United States.

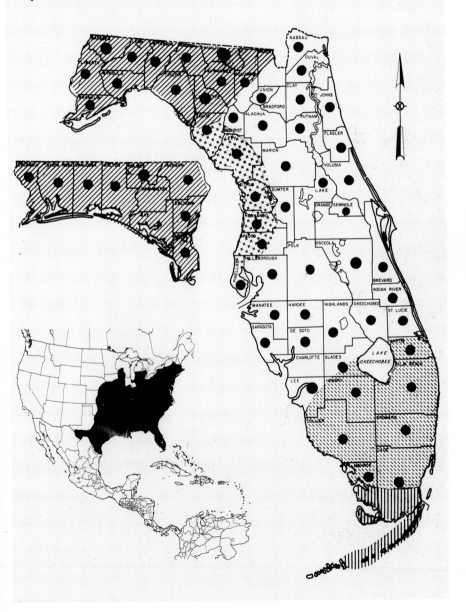

adult eastern mud snake

Farancia abacura abacura (Holbrook) **Eastern Mud Snake**

Description: This large, shiny snake, reaching a maximum length of 81 inches (205 cm), is named for its habitat and not its color. The glossy back is jet black with red or orange red triangular-shaped bars extending onto the sides from the belly. The head is black, and the eyes are tiny. The chin is yellow to yellow orange, spotted with black. The belly is red with broad patches of black. *The tip of the tail has a sharp pointed scale.*

Juveniles: Similar in form to the adults, their color is generally the same though occasionally red bands are present across the back.

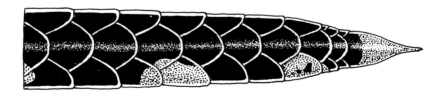

sharp tail tip—eastern mud snake

The Snakes—Colubrids

juvenile eastern mud snake

Similar Species: The rainbow snake has red stripes down the back and two rows of square-like spots on the belly. The smaller black swamp snake has neither red on the sides or back, nor black patches on the belly.

Natural History: This beautiful snake is found in shallow aquatic habitats including marshes, swamps, bogs, wet prairies, and bay heads. It is active at night, burrowing through detritus and mud in search for its favorite food—sirens and amphiuma. Most mud snakes are seen only on rainy nights while crossing roads. During the day, they remain burrowed in the mud or in aquatic vegetation. The sharp scale on the tip of the tail may be used to prod the slippery prey down the throat of the snake. Occasionally, when being handled, the mud snake will stick the handler with the sharp tail. Many people erroneously believe that this modified scale is a poisonous stinger.

Mud snakes cope moderately well in captivity if provided with prefered food—amphiuma, sirens, or eels. Occasionally individuals will eat tadpoles.

Reproduction: Adult mud snakes are among the few snake species that remain with and tend their eggs in the nest. Between 11-104 elliptical white eggs have been found in underground flask-shaped nests. The large number of eggs may be the product of more than one female—which may share the same nest. Eggs hatch in 60-80 days, usually in late summer.

The Snakes—Colubrids

Range of the Eastern Mud Snake in Florida is designated by dots within the counties. Insert map shows general distribution of the species in the United States.

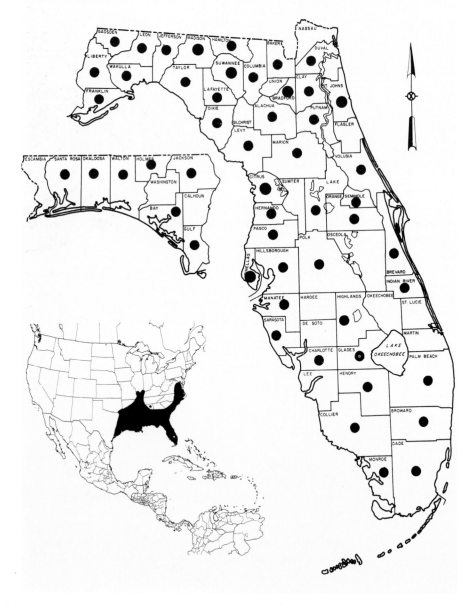

rainbow snake

Farancia erytrogramma erytrogramma (Palisot de Beauvois)
Rainbow Snake

Description: This medium-sized snake may reach a maximum length of 66 inches (168 cm). The rainbow snake gets its name from the highly iridescent scales. The back is dark gray to black with three red, longitudinal stripes. *The underside is yellow to flesh colored with a broad red stripe down the center, bordered on either side by a row of large black dots.* The head is small with yellow lips and small eyes.

Juveniles: Similar to adults in form and coloration.

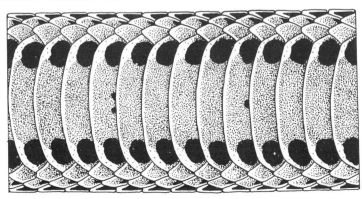

belly pattern—rainbow snake

Similar Species: The mud snake and the black swamp snake lack dorsal stripes.

Natural History: Although found in similar habitats as the mud snake, the rainbow snake tends to occur most often in spring runs, clear streams, and rivers, often found in mats of vegetation along the shoreline. It is occasionally

Range of the Rainbow Snake in Florida is designated by the open area, South Florida Rainbow Snake by the ⊙ area. Insert map shows general distribution of the species in the United States.

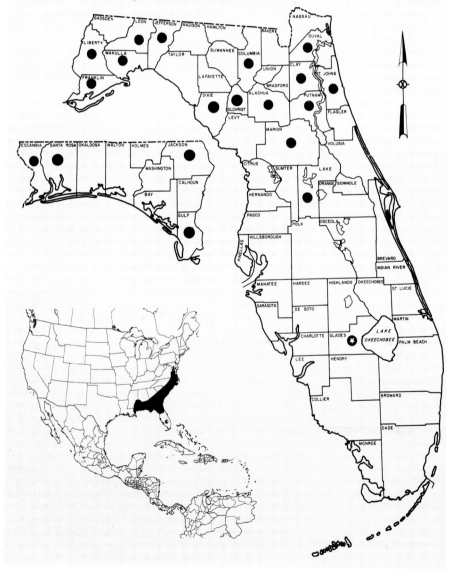

The Snakes—Colubrids

encountered when digging or plowing; sometimes, they are found crossing roads at night during or following a rain storm. The rainbow snake apparently feeds on amphiuma, sirens, fish, eels, and tadpoles. Juveniles have been reported to eat earthworms.

Like the mud snake, the rainbow snake has a sharp but harmless spine at the end of its tail. Both snakes are often called hoop snakes because of an old legendary tale that these snakes take their tail in their mouth and roll after the intended victim. This story is, of course, false. The rainbow snake is very docile and rarely if ever bites, nor is the tail poisonous.

Reproduction: Between 22-52 eggs are laid in sandy soil. Eggs are laid in late spring or early summer, hatching occurs in about 80 days. The young remain in or around the nest for some time.

Subspecies: *Farancia erytrogramma seminola* (Neill) **South Florida Rainbow Snake** This race resembles the rainbow snake except that the black blotches on the belly are larger and extend onto the sides.

Heterodon platyrhinos Latreille
Eastern Hognose Snake

Description: This medium-sized snake may reach a length of up to 45 inches (115 cm). The snake is highly variable in color. Some individuals are uniformly black or charcoal in color. Others are gray with faint blotches of darker gray. Still others are yellowish orange in color with dark brown or black blotches. *The underside is gray or greenish gray, and the underside of the tail is lighter.* This snake is best identified by the large upturned scale on the snout and by the large head.

JIM BRIDGES

Note upturned rostra of eastern hognose snake.

black phase eastern hognose snake   yellow phase eastern hognose snake

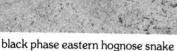

Juveniles: The young of all the color phases have dark blotches on a gray background, similar to the southern hognose.

Similar Species: The southern hognose has a light belly and undersurface of the tail. The snout is more upturned.

Natural History: This species often known as the puff adder, blow adder or puffer, gets its name from one of its many unusual defensive behaviors. When alarmed, a hognose will spread its head and neck and hiss loudly. While hissing, the snake may strike, but with its mouth closed. If provoked further, it will go into fake convulsions, often accompanied by regurgitation of food and defecation. Finally, it will lie limp, upside down, feigning death. Even when picked up, the snake will persist in playing dead. However, when place upright, the eastern hognose will immediately flip over on its back. After being handled for a while, this snake will refrain from such behavior.

The hognose snake is found primarily in dry, sandy habitats, pine flatwoods, xeric hammocks, or longleaf pine-turkey oak.

82   The Snakes—Colubrids

The hognose feeds primarily on frogs and toads but will occasionally eat small mice.

Reproduction: Six to 39 white eggs are laid in sandy soil, usually in early summer. Eggs hatch in late July-August, about 60 days after being laid.

Range of the Eastern Hognose Snake in Florida. Insert map shows general distribution of the species in the United States.

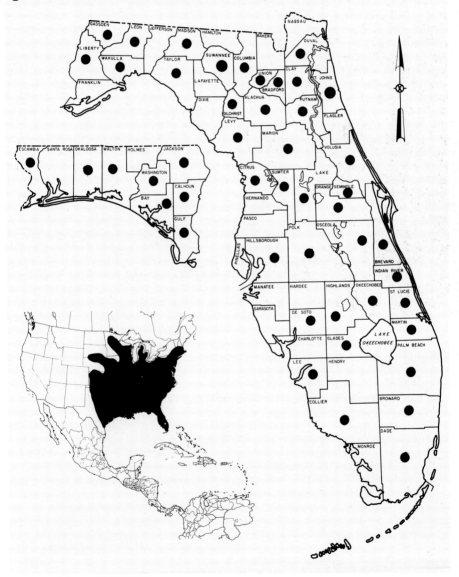

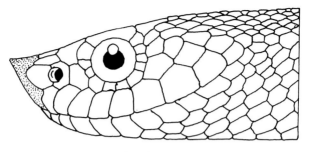

eastern hognose

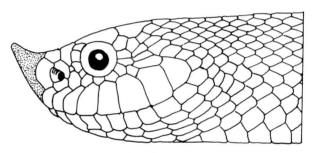

southern hognose

compare upturned snouts

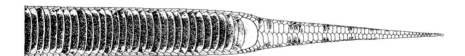

underside of tail—eastern hognose

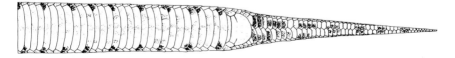

underside of tail—southern hognose

The Snakes—Colubrids

Heterodon simus (Linnaeus) **Southern Hognose Snake**

Description: This small chubby snake, reaching a maximum length of 24 inches (61 cm), is gray to gray brown with irregular or square-like blotches down the center and on the sides of the back. *The belly and underside of the tail are light gray or yellowish.* The large scale on the snout is more pointed and upturned than in the eastern hognose.

Juveniles: The young are similar to the adults.

Similar Species: The eastern hognose has a smaller, less upturned scale on the snout and the underside of the tail is lighter than the belly.

Natural History: The southern hognose inhabits the same sandy soil habitats as the eastern hognose, however, it has affinities for the more xeric habitats such as sand pine, or longleaf pine-turkey oak habitats. It has the same unusual defensive behavior as the eastern hognose. Both species have enlarged rear teeth. There is no proof that hognose snakes are poisonous. Apparently these teeth are used to deflate toads and frogs that puff up when seized by the snake. The southern hognose feeds primarily on frogs and toads, including spadefoots and treefrogs.

Reproduction: Little information is available on reproduction in this species. One author reported a female laying 9 eggs in mid-July, another reported 6 eggs being laid in October. The eggs are rounded and white.

JOHN B. IVERSON

southern hognose snake

Range of the Southern Hognose Snake in Florida. Insert map shows general distribution of the species in the United States.

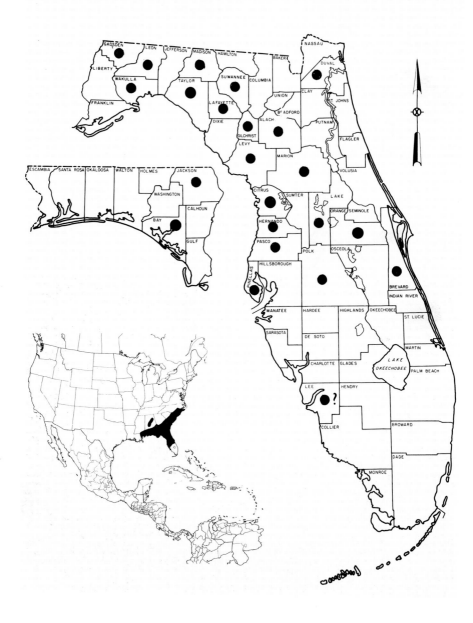

The Snakes—Colubrids

Lampropeltis calligaster rhombomaculata (Holbrook)
Mole Kingsnake

Description: This very rare snake attains a maximum length of 45 inches (115 cm). Like other kingsnakes, it has smooth scales. The back is generally a uniform brown to gray brown. Some specimens have reddish brown blotches down the center of the back and on each side. The blotches on the neck may be oblong; the head is usually uniformly tan.

Juveniles: Similar to adults except the blotches are more pronounced and are brown to red brown. The small head is not much wider than the neck.

Similar Species: The corn snake has a black and white checkered belly while the mole kingsnake has a yellowish white belly, lightly spotted or checked with brown.

Natural History: This snake spends most of its time underground and is rarely found except when it crosses roadways at night. Very little is known about the behavior of this snake. It feeds on lizards, small snakes, and small mammals. It will do moderately well in captivity if provided the same cage facilities described for the scarlet snake.

Reproduction: No natural nests are known. Eggs are probably laid underground.

R.W. VAN DEVENDER

gray color phase (most typical) mole kingsnake

tan color phase mole kingsnake

red color phase mole kingsnake

The Snakes—Colubrids

Range of the Mole Kingsnake in Florida. Insert map shows general distribution of the species in the United States.

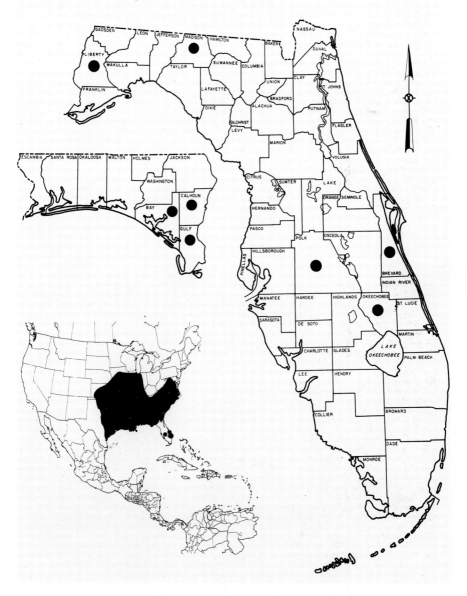

Lampropeltis getulus (Linnaeus) **Common Kingsnake**

Description: This snake reaches a maximum length of 82 inches (208 cm). Several races are recognized in Florida; all share the following characteristics: scales smooth and glossy, head and neck about the same diameter, chin scales barred with black and yellow.

Juveniles: They are similar to adults. The young of some of the lighter phases are darker than the parents while others are marked with orange or reddish markings not found in the adults.

Similar Species: Pine snakes have keeled scales and a large scale on the snout. Rat snakes lack the bars on the chin scales.

Natural History: These diverse snakes are well known for their immunity to snake venom and their appetite for other snakes, including the poisonous ones. Some poisonous snakes defend themselves in a strange manner when confronted by a kingsnake. The threatened poisonous snake will coil up, hiding its head in the middle of the coils. When the kingsnake approaches, the snake will raise part of its body in the air and then slam the raised part down on the ground or the kingsnake. If the body slams against the head of the probing kingsnake, it will usually withdraw temporarily. Kingsnakes also feed on lizards, birds, and small mammals. If cornered, they will strike, but when picked up, kingsnakes will casually turn to a finger and begin chewing. They usually tame in captivity but must be kept in cages by themselves. Also, cages must be kept dry and well ventilated, because kingsnakes are quite susceptible to skin disease. They are found in areas such as canal banks or under trash at the edge of wetlands.

JIM BRIDGES

eastern kingsnake

The Snakes—Colubrids

RAY E. ASHTON, JR.

juvenile Florida kingsnake

JIM BRIDGES

adult Florida kingsnake

ED CASSANO

color variant—south Florida kingsnake

The Snakes—Colubrids

Reproduction: Mating occurs in the spring, with up to 17 oval, white eggs laid in early to middle summer, probably in rotten logs or in burrows of small mammals. Eggs hatch in two months.

Subspecies:

It should be noted that kingsnake taxonomy is poorly understood. In Florida, currently only *L. getulus getulus* and *L. getulus floridana* are recognized subspecies occuring in the state.

Lampropeltis getulus getulus (Linnaeus) **Eastern Kingsnake** This subspecies is generally black to chocolate brown with a cream-to-yellow chain or net-like pattern over the back. In some populations, the chain pattern is quite wide, giving the appearance of large dark blotches down the center and the sides of the back. The belly is yellow with cream to yellow square-like blotches.

Lampropeltis getulus floridana Blanchard **Florida Kingsnake** This subspecies has many small black or brown blotches surrounded by white or cream. Another color phase, considered by some as a separate race, has very light tan blotches surrounded by light markings. This color phase occurs in the Apalachicola and Okefenokee regions. The dorsal scales on this color phase are edged in black. The belly is yellow to cream with black square-like blotches.

Color Variants:

South Florida Kingsnake This is another color phase found in south Florida that is considered by many as a separate race. The snake is mostly cream white with little or no blotching. The dorsal scales are edged in black, and the underside is cream with faint gray spots. Some herpetologists believe this race is highly specialized in preying upon turtle eggs.

Blotched Kingsnake This color phase is found only in the Chipola and Appalachicola River Valleys of the Florida panhandle. This form has very wide yellow bands and less than 25 blotches on the back.

JIM BRIDGES

color variant—blotched kingsnake

The Snakes—Colubrids

Range of the Common Kingsnake in Florida. Insert map shows general distribution of *Lampropeltis getulus* **in the United States.**

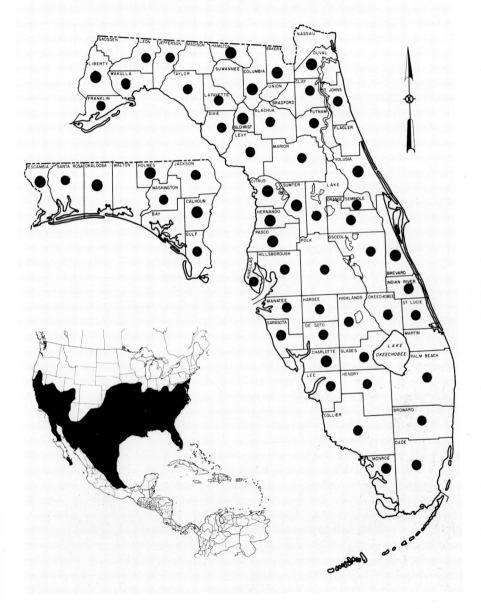

Lampropeltis triangulum elapsoides (Holbrook)
Scarlet Kingsnake

Description: This small, colorful, banded serpent is a coral snake mimic. The bands run completely around the body, the red bands are usually broad and are bordered by black with wider yellow bands between the black. *The snout is usually red and somewhat pointed.* The scales are smooth and shiny. This small kingsnake reaches a maximum length of 27 inches (68 cm).

Juveniles: Similar to adults.

Similar Species: The poisonous coral snake has a black snout. The broad red bands are bordered by narrow yellow bands with wide black bands between them on the coral snake. The scarlet snake has a white belly.

Natural History: The scarlet kingsnake is rarely seen except on highways at night. Collectors find them in pine stumps in wet areas during the winter. Occasionally they are exposed during plowing or when fire lanes are being dug. This snake feeds on small lizards and snakes. In captivity, larger individuals will eat small mice. They are often difficult to maintain in captivity, refusing to eat, but can be kept with some degree of success if the snake is given some cover to hide under and a steady supply of live ground skinks or anoles.

Reproduction: The author has observed breeding in mid-April. Up to six elongated white eggs are laid in late spring to midsummer. Eggs hatch in 60-75 days.

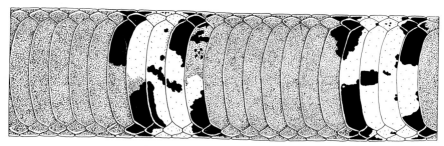

belly pattern—scarlet kingsnake

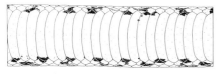

belly pattern—scarlet snake

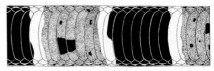

belly pattern—coral snake

The Snakes—Colubrids

Range of the Scarlet Kingsnake in Florida. Insert map shows distribution of the race in the United States.

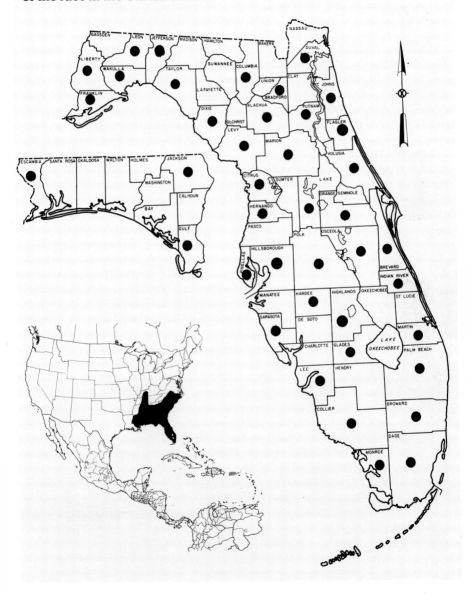

common color phase—scarlet kingsnake

yellow color phase—scarlet kingsnake

The Snakes—Colubrids

Note red pointed snout of scarlet kingsnake.

Masticophis flagellum flagellum (Shaw) **Eastern Coachwhip**

Description: This large, impressive snake, reaching a length of 102 inches (260 cm), may vary greatly in color. The large smooth scales on the back may be black from the head to approximately one-half of the total length. The black coloring blends into a tan, then cream on the tail, giving the animal a braided look, similar to a whip. Other individuals may be a uniform tan color or some may be all black. The undersides also can vary in color. Some may be brown or gray on the chin and belly, changing to cream color on the underside of the tail. Some individuals may have four faint stripes on the throat which extend down to mid-belly. The eyes and head are large.

Juveniles: The young are brown or tan with dark irregular bands. Juvenile black racers are gray with rusty blotches.

Similar Species: The black racer has large smooth scales, a dark underside, and a uniformly dark back.

Natural History: This large, active, diurnal snake is a relatively common inhabitant of dry (xeric) habitats with open understories. These habitats include pine flatwoods, longleaf pine-turkey oak, and sand pine scrub. The coachwhip is

The Snakes—Colubrids   97

Range of the Eastern Coachwhip in Florida. Insert map shows general distribution of the race in the United States.

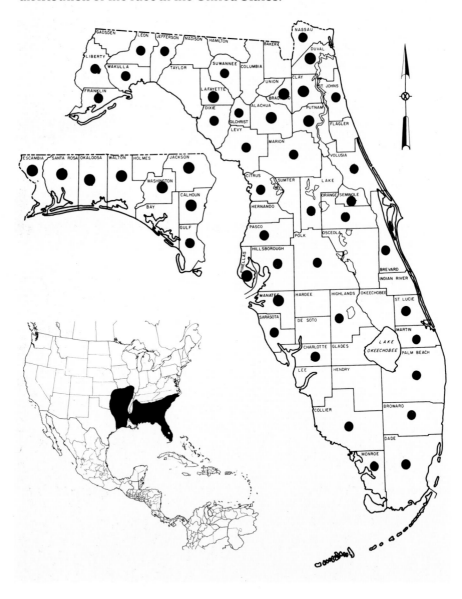

The Snakes—Colubrids

dark phase eastern coachwhip

light phase eastern coachwhip in defensive posture

The Snakes—Colubrids

juvenile eastern coachwhip

an excellent climber and can travel on the ground at great speeds, making it very difficult to capture. When captured, it will defend itself with tearing bites.

It feeds on lizards, other snakes, small mammals, and birds. An individual engaged in the hunt, observed by the author, was crawling in short spurts with the head held erect, pausing to look up at low trees, almost systematically checking each one for movement of possible prey. Finally, the coachwhip located a fence lizard, which it captured in a flurry of speed, grabbing the lizard from the base of the tree in its powerful jaws.

The coachwhip remains nervous and often refuses food in captivity. They may survive if provided a very large cage with a basking area, and a diet of live lizards and small rodents.

Reproduction: A clutch of 12-16 eggs is laid in the late spring or early summer. The eggs are elongated, white and have a rough surface. Breeding probably takes place as soon as the snake becomes active in spring. Little is known about coachwhip reproduction in Florida.

Nerodia cyclopion floridana (Goff)
Florida Green Water Snake

Description: This large, ill-tempered but nonpoisonous water snake reaches a maximum length of 55 inches (140 cm) and is uniform olive green to greenish brown in color. Some individuals in south Florida are rusty red. *The belly is cream color with no markings.* The dorsal scales are keeled. The teeth are long, even in the young.

Florida green water snake

typical brown phase Florida green water snake

The Snakes—Colubrids

Juveniles: The young are greenish or brownish in color and are marked with numerous brown bands. The belly is yellow to cream with faint brown markings under the tail.

Similar Species: This snake is often confused with the poisonous cottonmouth; both frequent the same habitats. Cottonmouths are black or brown with white markings across the face. They also have vertical pupils and a

Range of the Florida Green Water Snake in Florida. Insert map shows general distribution of the species in the United States.

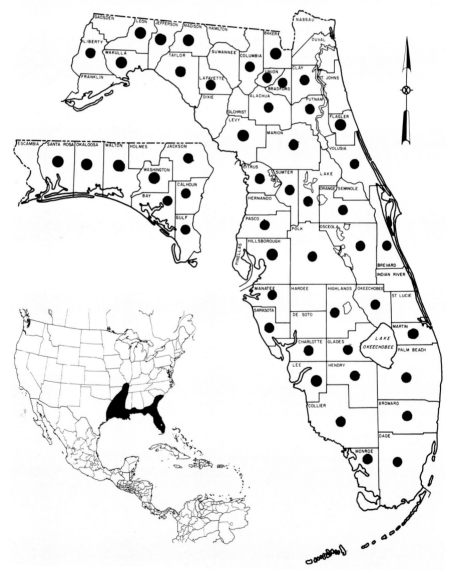

The Snakes—Colubrids

facial pit on each side of the head. Salt marsh snakes and banded water snakes have distinct markings on the belly.

Natural History: The green water snake is extremely common throughout Florida. It inhabits shallow lakes, ponds, marshes and roadside ditches with profuse floating vegetation. Like most water snakes, it basks along the grassy edges or in branches overhanging rivers, lakes or swamps. When alarmed, it will drop into the water and disappear under the aquatic vegetation. Green water snakes are often seen crossing roads at night. When cornered or caught, this species can inflict a painful bite. Unlike most snakes which make simple puncture wounds, these snakes may inflict deep lacerations. Even juveniles can bite severely. Like other water snakes, they will release large amounts of feces and foul smelling musk when provoked. Surprisingly, these water snakes become docile and make relatively good pets, readily taking frogs and fish. In the wild, they also feed on salamanders, tadpoles, small turtles, and invertebrates.

A water snake in captivity should be kept separate from other snakes because they sometimes harbor parasitic diseases that may prove harmful to other species.

Reproduction: Breeding probably takes place in early spring. Between 8-100 young are born in midsummer. Clutch size depends on age and size of the female. Large gravid females may weigh up to ten pounds.

Nerodia erythrogaster erythrogaster (Forster)
Redbelly Water Snake

Description: The rough-scaled back of this attractive snake is usually a plain greenish blue, becoming lighter blue on the sides. Some individuals are brown with bluish gray on the sides. The throat is yellowish to orange which turns into an *orange red on the belly.* Both upper and lower lips may be reddish or yellow red in color. The top of the head may be brown to gray blue. The redbelly water snake may reach a length of 62 inches (157.5 cm).

Juveniles: Young are strongly patterned with three rows of irregular blotches on the body, and the belly is creamy yellow. Occasionally reddish individuals may have narrow black borders along the edge of the belly scales.

Similar Species: Black swamp snakes are always black on the back. All other water snakes occuring in the same areas that have plain bellies have markings on the back.

Natural History: The redbelly water snake is most common along large rivers, usually basking in overhanging bushes or on the bank. The species is uncommon in Florida. A very shy snake, it will drop or shoot into the water at the slightest provocation. Often redbelly water snakes will share the same basking site with brown and banded water snakes.

The redbelly water snake eats frogs, fish, tadpoles, crayfish and aquatic invertebrates. In captivity, it feeds well on frogs, toads, minnows, or frozen fish, and will often calm down and refrain from biting and exuding musk when handled.

Reproduction: Breeding apparently begins in early spring and continues

The Snakes—Colubrids

through early summer. About 16 young are born alive from midsummer to early fall.

   Subspecies: *Nerodia erythrogaster flavigaster* Conant **Yellowbelly Water Snake** This panhandle race has a belly that is yellow to yellow orange in color.

Range of the Redbelly Water Snake in Florida is designated by the open area, Yellowbelly Water Snake by the ▨ area. Insert map shows general distribution of *Nerodia erythrogaster* in the United States.

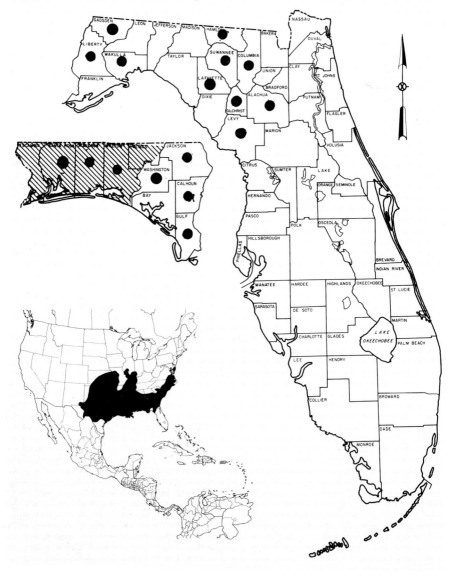

The Snakes—Colubrids

juvenile redbelly water snake

adult redbelly water snake

The Snakes—Colubrids

Nerodia fasciata pictiventris (Cope) **Florida Water Snake**

Description: This medium-sized water snake, reaching a length of 63 inches (159 cm), is banded with broad dark bands across the back. The lighter, narrower bands are tan to reddish. In some dark individuals, the bands are difficult to see. The belly is creamy yellow, and each scute is edged with brown or red. A dark stripe occurs from the eye to the corner of the jaw. The scales are rough and dull.

Juveniles: The bands are very clear and bright. Belly patterns are similar to adults.

Similar Species: This snake is often confused with the poisonous cottonmouth which has a much thicker, broad head with facial pits. Also, the bands on the cottonmouth are much broader.

Natural History: This is one of the most common species of snakes in Florida. It inhabits nearly all aquatic habitats, where it is often seen sunning on the banks or overhanging vegetation. It is frequently seen at night, especially after rains, often when crossing roads that come near water. It feeds on live or dead

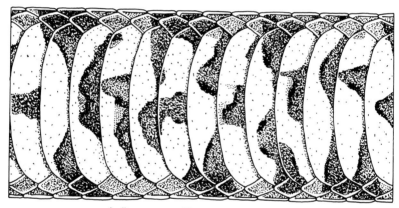

belly pattern—Florida water snake

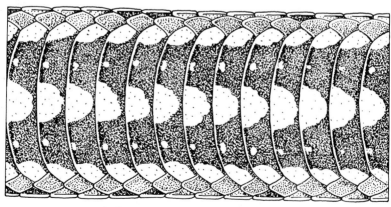

belly pattern—Gulf salt marsh snake

The Snakes—Colubrids

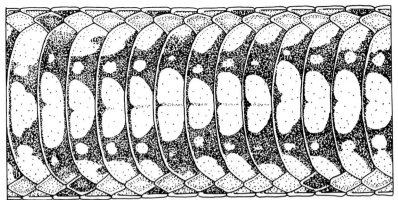

belly pattern—Atlantic salt marsh snake

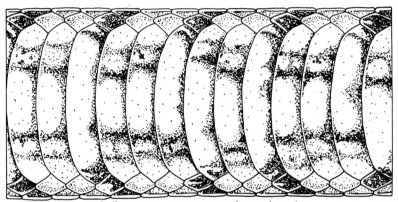

belly pattern—mangrove salt marsh snake

Gulf salt marsh snake

The Snakes—Colubrids

Range of the Florida Water Snake in Florida is designated by the open area, Banded Water Snake by the ▨ area, Gulf Salt Marsh Snake by the ⋮⋮⋮ area, Atlantic Salt Marsh Snake by the ░ area, and Mangrove Salt Marsh Snake by the ◉ area. Insert map shows general distribution of *Nerodia fasciata* in the United States.

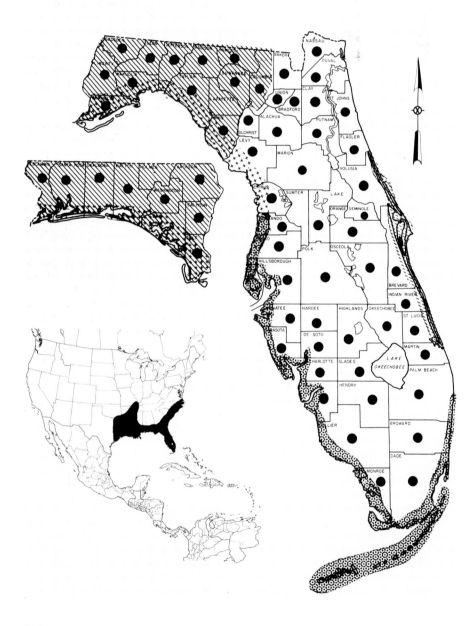

The Snakes—Colubrids

Florida water snake

Florida water snake

fish, frogs, toads, aquatic invertebrates. When captured, it bites savagely and spurts foul smelling musk. It may do well in captivity on a diet of fish and frogs, but usually retains its pugnacious behavior.

Reproduction: Breeding may occur in the fall to early spring, with young born in the late spring or early summer. More than 50 live young may be born at one time.

The Snakes—Colubrids   109

Subspecies:

Nerodia fasciata fasciata (Linnaeus) **Banded Water Snake** This subspecies resembles the Florida water snake, except the belly is marked with irregular or square-like blotches.

Nerodia fasciata clarki (Baird and Girard) **Gulf Salt Marsh Snake** *Description:* This medium-sized snake, reaching a length of 36 inches (91 cm), is the only striped water snake living in brackish or salt marshes. There are four longitudinal stripes on each side, two are dull tan, and two dark brown to grayish. The belly is brown to reddish with a creamy yellow stripe extending down the center. The scales are heavily keeled. *Juveniles:* Similar to adults but the stripes are brighter. *Similar Species:* Garter snakes have three stripes on the back and a plain belly. Other water snakes are banded or blotched. *Natural History:* This salt marsh snake is common on coastal marshes and offshore islands. It is rare in fresh water. It feeds primarily on small fish, but small invertebrates such as crabs are included in its diet as well. When first captured, this snake may bite, but it usually becomes docile. Rarely seen during the day, the salt marsh snake forages for food at night. Most other snakes can only tolerate salt water for short periods of time. *Reproduction:* Breeding probably occurs in early spring. Litters average about 11-12; young are born alive, probably during middle to late summer.

Nerodia fasciata taeniata Cope **Atlantic Salt Marsh Snake** This snake is striped almost to the middle of the body, where the stripes fade and the markings are bands or blotches. Patterns vary greatly in all of the salt marsh snakes, so the maps should be consulted for the most likely subspecies. This subspecies is considered to be threatened throughout its range.

Nerodia fasciata compressicauda (Kennicott) **Mangrove Salt Marsh Snake** *Description:* This medium-sized water snake is extremely variable in color and reaches a maximum length of 37 inches (94 cm). Commonly they are brownish to gray with faint dark blotches or crossbands on the back. The neck usually has two light stripes on either side. The head is normally brown or gray. Some individuals are uniformly rusty red to dull yellow. The belly of the brown or

orange color phase mangrove salt marsh snake

The Snakes—Colubrids

ROBERT S. SIMMONS

common gray phase mangrove salt marsh snake

WILLIAM B. and KATHLEEN V. LOVE

rusty color phase mangrove salt marsh snake

The Snakes—Colubrids

gray individual is yellowish, peppered with brown or reddish dots. These dots may form an irregular stripe down the center of the belly. Reddish individuals have a yellowish belly washed with red. *Similar Species:* This is the only water snake that occurs in the brackish mangrove swamps. The cottonmouth has broad bands across the back and a dark broad head. *Juveniles:* They are similar to adults but have more conspicuous banding or blotching. *Natural History:* The mangrove salt marsh snake inhabits the black and red mangrove swamps, canals and brackish swamps along the southern shores of Florida. This race feeds most often on small minnows and invertebrates that are common in these habitats. *Reproduction:* Breeding probably takes place in late winter and early spring. About 11 young are born alive during the summer. There is some indication that this subspecies may also produce spring broods.

Nerodia taxispilota (Holbrook) **Brown Water Snake**

Description: This large—up to 69 inches (175 cm)—heavy bodied snake is dull brown with 3 rows of dark brown, square-like blotches, usually bordered by light lines. Often, in larger specimens, the blotches are obscure. The large head is brown with few or no markings. The underside is creamy yellow with a heavy patterns of square-like brown blotches. The scales are rough and dull.

Juveniles: The young are similar to adults, but more brightly colored.

Similar Species: The Florida green water snake lacks the large square-like blotches and its underside is a uniform color. Young Florida and midland water snakes may resemble the brown watersnake, but they both lack the heavily blotched belly.

JACK DERMID

brown water snake

The Snakes—Colubrids

Natural History: This common water snake is found around rivers, lakes, and large ponds. It is often seen sunning on exposed banks and overhanging shrubs and trees. The brown water snake has a foul disposition and will bite ferociously. Its bite, like the Florida green water snake, can be extremely painful. Unlike most nonpoisonous snakes that inflict small puncture wounds, the brown water snake may inflict slash wounds or cuts when it bites.

Range of the Brown Water Snake in Florida. Insert map shows general distribution of the species in the United States.

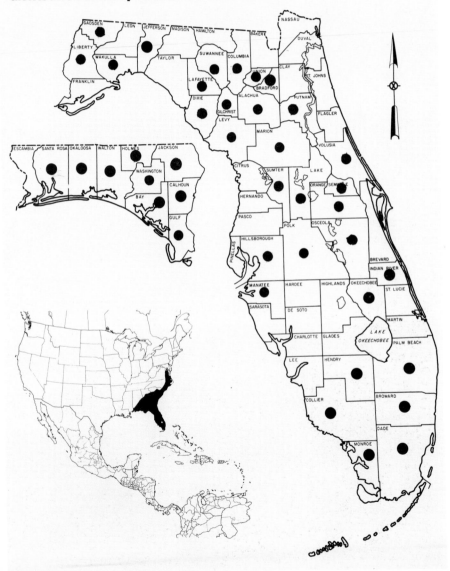

Its diet consists of fish, frogs, other small vertebrates, and invertebrates.

In captivity, this species does well and may even become docile. Some microscopic parasites of these and other water snakes may be harmful to other species in captivity. Therefore, it is wise to keep these snakes in separate cages.

Reproduction: Breeding occurs in middle to late summer and as many as 30-40 young are born in late summer.

Nerodia sipedon pleuralis (Cope) **Midland Water Snake**

Description: This heavy bodied snake is gray brown to reddish or dark brown and reaches a maximum length of 51 inches (131 cm). The back is banded anteriorly. At about midbody, the bands change into square-like blotches. The underside is creamy yellow with *two rows of crescent shaped brown to reddish brown markings* extending from the chin onto the tail.

belly pattern—midland water snake

ROBERT H. MOUNT

midland water snake

114   The Snakes—Colubrids

Juveniles: The young are similar to adults, but the pattern is brighter.

Similar Species: The Florida water snake has bands along the entire upper surface, and its underside is marked with irregular blotches. The redbelly water snake has a plain belly.

Natural History: The midland water snake only occurs in the extreme western panhandle area in the Escambia, Yellow and Choctawhatchee rivers. It feeds on small fish, frogs, and invertebrates.

Range of the Midland Water Snake in Florida. Insert map shows general distribution of the species in the United States.

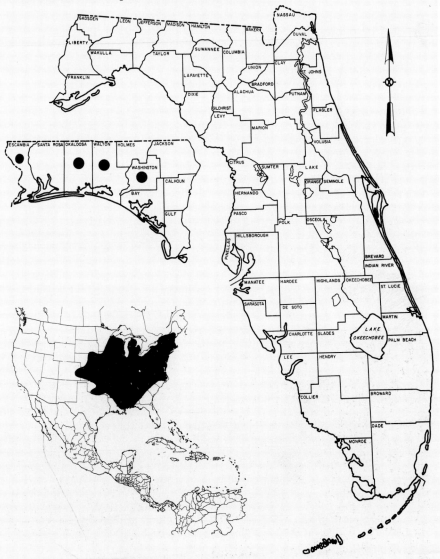

When alarmed, it flattens its head and body and strikes repeatedly. Many people confuse this water snake with the poisonous water moccasin. This snake does well in captivity on a diet of fish and frogs, but usually maintains a foul disposition.

Reproduction: Breeding probably takes place in early spring. Approximately 26-46 young are born alive in late summer.

Opheodrys aestivus   (Linnaeus)   **Rough Green Snake**

Description: This species may reach a length of more than 46 inches (116 cm). It is a very slender, keel-scaled snake with a bright green back and a cream to yellow belly.

Juveniles: The young are similar in appearance and coloration to the adults, but they are somewhat grayer.

Similar Species: This is the only slender, bright green snake native to Florida. However, the tropical vine snake, *Oxybelis,* has been reported as a released species in Dade County. This mildly poisonous, rear-fanged species has a very slender head and pointed snout. Usually the sides of the tropical vine snake are pinkish to buff in color and the scales are smooth.

Natural History: The green snake is very common throughout Florida. It may be found in moist habitats, living in shrubs and low growing vegetation often at the edge of lakes, ponds, and rivers. The green camouflage color makes this species extremely difficult to see. This mild-mannered species will rarely bite and when confronted by danger will usually move a short distance along a branch and then freeze, relying on its camouflage for protection. It feeds on spiders, moths,

ED CASSANO

rough green snake

The Snakes—Colubrids

tree crickets, and other soft-bodied invertebrates. Although sold in pet stores, this species does not adapt to captivity very well.

Reproduction: Three to 12 elongate, white eggs are laid between middle and late summer, usually under objects in damp areas. The eggs hatch in late summer or fall. Some individuals may carry eggs over winter and lay them in early spring.

Range of the Rough Green Snake in Florida. Insert map shows general distribution of the species in the United States.

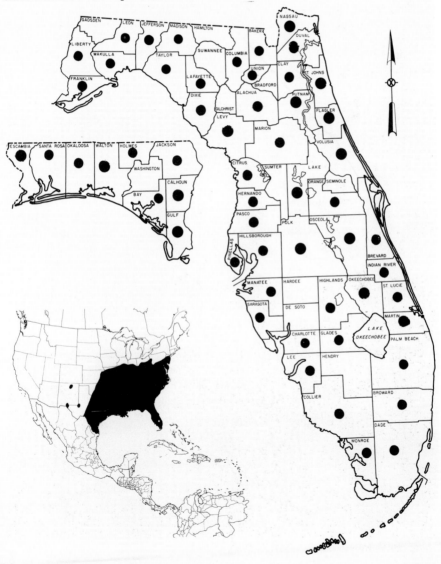

Pituophis melanoleucus mugitus   Barbour
Florida Pine Snake

Description: This large stocky snake is highly variable in color and reaches a maximum length of 90 inches (228 cm). The background color is usually ashy gray. The back is saddled with dark tan to reddish blotches. These blotches may be absent in some individuals, giving the snake an almost albino appearance. In others, the blotches may be nearly black. The blotches become brick red bands as they approach the tail. The underside is uniformly smoky gray. The snout is covered by a large triangular-shaped scale. The scales are keeled.

Juveniles: The young are similar to adults except that the pattern is much brighter.

Similar Species: Gray rat snakes lack an enlarged scale on the snout and bands across the tail. Their scales are also smooth or very weakly keeled.

RAY E. ASHTON, JR.

Note enlarged rostral scale of Florida pine snake.

RAY E. ASHTON, JR.

Florida pine snake

The Snakes—Colubrids

Natural History: Next to the hognose, the pine snake is one of the best actors in the snake world. When alarmed, the snake will swell up and hiss very loudly. The loud hiss is produced by the exhaled air being passed over a flap of tissue that stretches across the air opening in the mouth. Pine snakes, unlike the hognose snakes, will bite. They live in sandy habitats, particularly longleaf pine-turkey oak where the pocket gopher is commonly found. Their diet consists of pocket gophers and other small mammals as well as birds which they kill by

Range of the Florida Pine Snake in Florida. Insert map shows general distribution of the subspecies in the United States.

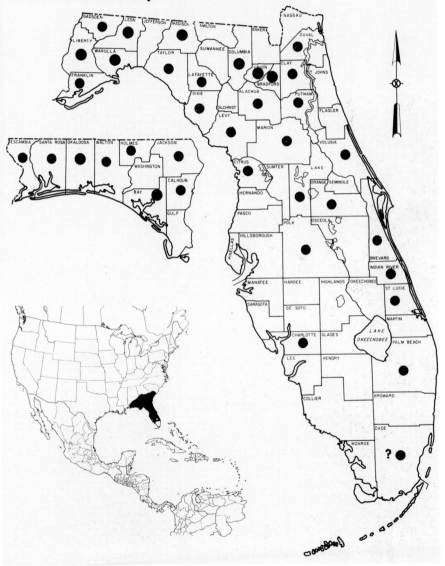

constriction. Young pine snakes will eat race runners and other lizards. This species usually does quite well in captivity, however, some individuals will remain nervous and refuse to eat.

Florida pine snake populations appear to be on the decline in many areas of the state, apparently due to habitat destruction.

Reproduction: Breeding probably occurs in early spring, possibly in the winter in some southern localities. Approximately 8 large, white eggs are laid during middle to late summer, probably in gopher *(Geomys)* burrows. Little is known about reproduction in this subspecies.

Regina alleni (Garman) **Striped Crayfish Snake**

Description: This semi-glossy snake is brownish above with three very faint darker stripes on the back. The lower sides are yellow to creamy yellow with thin faint brown stripes; *belly is plain and yellow to orange colored.* This snake reaches a maximum size of 26 inches (65 cm).

Juveniles: Similar to adults.

Similar Species: The glossy water snake has two rows of half moons on the belly, while the queen snake has four stripes on the belly.

Natural History: The striped crayfish snake is found most often among the roots of water hyacinths in swamps, ponds, lakes, and slow moving rivers. Originally, it probably was an inhabitant of mats of floating vegetation and floating islands. The snake may wander onto roads during or just after evening rains. It is highly specialized, feeding entirely on crayfish, which it captures by en-

JIM BRIDGES

striped crayfish snake

The Snakes—Colubrids

circling the prey with coils, similar to the method used by the rat snake and other constrictors. It doesn't crush or suffocate the crayfish, but rather holds it in place while swallowing it. Young crayfish snakes may eat dragonfly larvae and other aquatic invertebrates. The crayfish snake does poorly in captivity, refusing food, and is very susceptible to skin diseases.

Reproduction: Breeding probably takes place in the spring, and an average of 10 young are born alive between May and September.

Range of the Striped Crayfish Snake in Florida. Insert map shows general distribution of the species in the United States.

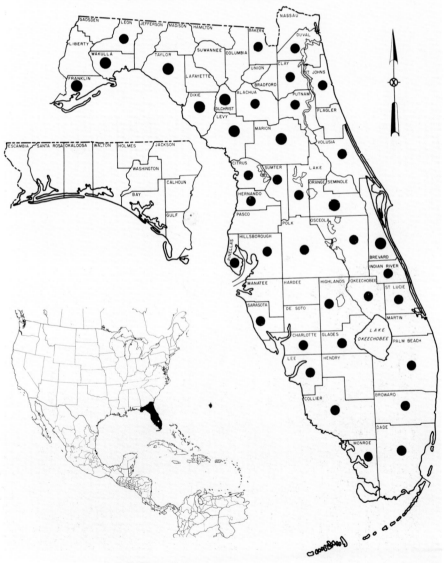

Regina rigida rigida   (Say)   Glossy Crayfish Snake

Description: This medium-sized crayfish snake is solid brown above with a thin dark "pin" stripe along each side. *The belly is cream to yellow with two rows of brown half moons.* It reaches a length of 31 inches (79 cm). There is a faint dusky stripe along each side of the throat.

Juveniles: The young are marked like the adults.

Similar Species: The black swamp snake is black above and lacks the rows of half moons on the belly. The queen snake, redbelly snake, and striped crayfish snake are brown above but lack the half moons on the belly.

Natural History: The glossy crayfish snake is very secretive and is seldom observed. Most specimens are collected crossing roads at night during heavy rains. Some are found underneath objects along the edge of the water. This

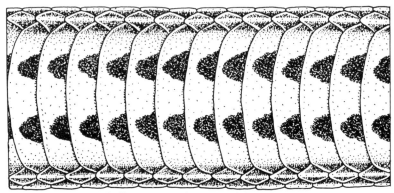

belly pattern—glossy crayfish snake

RAY E. ASHTON, JR.

glossy crayfish snake

The Snakes—Colubrids

species inhabits sphagnum swamps and small to medium size streams. It spends much time in the water. It feeds primarily on crayfish as an adult and small aquatic invertebrates such as dragonfly larvae when young. Small frogs, fish, and salamanders may also be taken.

This species is difficult to maintain in captivity. It often refuses to eat and seems very susceptible to skin diseases. When alarmed, it will flatten its head and body,

Range of the Glossy Crayfish Snake in Florida is designated by the open area, Gulf Crayfish Snake by the ▒ area. Insert map shows general distribution of *Regina rigida* in the United States.

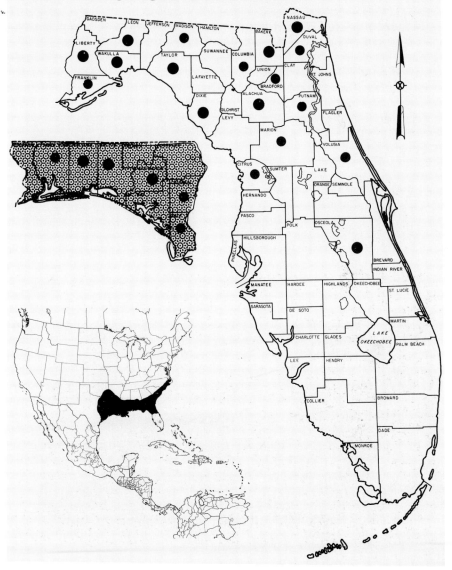

spread a foul musk, and may occasionally bite.

Reproduction: Mating probably occurs in April and May. About 16 young are born during summer.

Subspecies: *Regina rigida sinicola* (Huheey) **Gulf Crayfish Snake** Unlike the glossy crayfish snake, the Gulf crayfish snake does not have thin dusky lines on the side of the throat.

Regina septemvittata (Say) **Queen Snake**

Description: This medium-sized snake is dull olive brown to dark brown. *The belly is creamy yellow with four brown or tan stripes.* In adults, the head often appears small for the body. This snake reaches a maximum length of 36 inches (92 cm).

Juveniles: Juveniles are similar to adults.

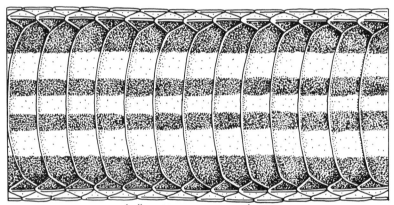

belly pattern—queen snake

ROBERT S. SIMMONS

queen snake

The Snakes—Colubrids

Similar Species: Glossy crayfish snake is shiny above, and the belly has two rows of half moons instead of stripes.

Natural History: The queen snake has a limited range in Florida but is rather common in the streams where it occurs. It inhabits small to medium size streams, usually with fast moving water. It often basks on shrubs and trees overhanging the water. It feeds almost entirely on crayfish and other aquatic

Range of the Queen Snake in Florida. Insert map shows general distribution of the species in the United States.

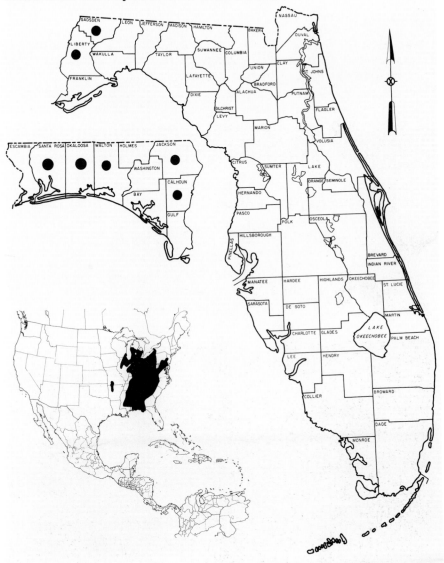

invertebrates, but will, on occasion take cricket frogs, tadpoles, and minnows. When first captured, the queen snake will flatten its small head and body and bite vigorously. It also releases a very strong smelling musk. After some handling, this snake refrains from biting but will remain nervous and refuse food in captivity. The queen snake is susceptible to skin diseases in captivity.

Reproduction: Breeding probably occurs from April to June. Young are born usually during middle to late summer. Eleven to 31 young have been reported in a single litter.

Rhadinaea flavilata (Cope) **Pine Woods Snake**

Description: A small colorful glossy snake that may be tan, yellow, brown, or orange ablve, the pine woods snake reaches a maximum length of 16 inches (40 cm). The belly is yellow. *There is a dark line from the snout, through the eye, to the angle of the jaw.* The lips and chin are cream to white with dark flecks. The head is larger than the neck; scales are smooth.

Juveniles: The young are similar to the adults.

Similar Species: Redbelly snakes have a bright red-orange or red belly, and a ring or three spots around the neck.

Natural History: The pine woods snake is the only North American representative of a group that occurs primarily in Central and South America. It is found in moist pine flatwoods near cypress heads or along the wooded edges of wet prairies. It feeds on salamanders, small frogs, and lizards. It has a mild venom and enlarged rear teeth. It is, however, harmless to man and makes no attempt to

RAY E. ASHTON, JR.

pine woods snake

　The Snakes—Colubrids

bite, even when first captured. The long slender tail of this species may break easily during capture.

The pine woods snake does moderately well in captivity if given cricket frogs, small treefrogs, or lizards.

Reproduction: Two to four elongate white eggs are laid during May to August.

Range of the Pine Woods Snake in Florida. Insert map shows general distribution of the species in the United States.

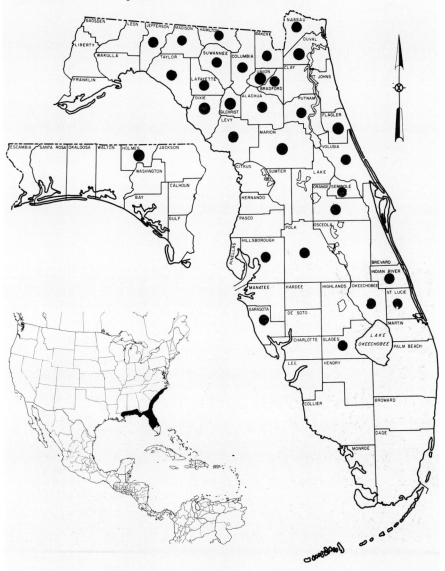

Seminatrix pygaea pygaea   (Cope)
North Florida Swamp Snake

Description: This small shiny black snake has smooth scales and grows to a length of 18 inches (47 cm). The chin is yellow to pink turning to strawberry red or *scarlet on the belly.* Each belly scale is notched with a small square-like black blotch.

Similar Species: The much larger mud snake has large blotches of black on the belly. The rainbow snake has red stripes on its belly.

Juveniles: Same as adults.

Natural History: This swamp snake is commonly found in the same aquatic vegetation as the striped crayfish snake. Before hyacinths were introduced into Florida waters, this beautiful snake probably inhabited decaying vegetation on the bottom of shallow marshes and cypress swamps where it can still be collected

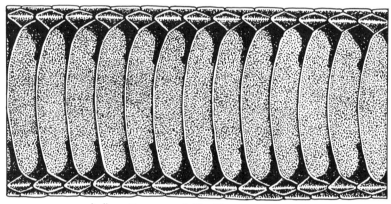

belly pattern—south Florida swamp snake

JIM BRIDGES

Florida swamp snake

The Snakes—Colubrids

today. In winter it burrows into bottom vegetation or sphagnum. This small snake feeds on small aquatic invertebrates and small salamanders.

The north Florida swamp snake does not do well in captivity.

Reproduction: Breeding may take place in both the early spring and fall with 6 young produced in the fall or late summer.

Range of the North Florida Swamp Snake in Florida is designated by the open area, South Florida Swamp Snake by the :::: area. Insert map shows general distribution of *Seminatrix pygaea* **in the United States.**

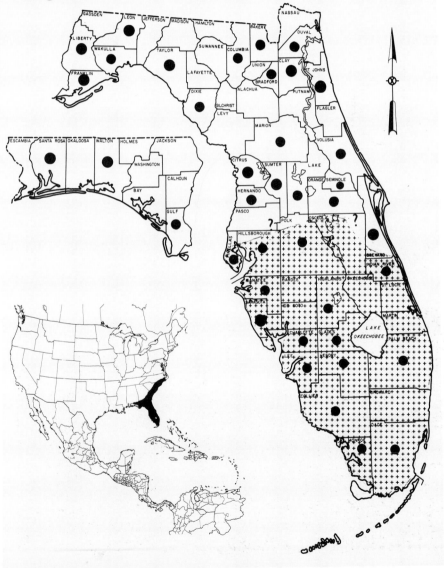

Subspecies: *Seminatrix pygaea cyclas* Dowling **South Florida Swamp Snake** This subspecies, which occurs in the southern half of Florida, is distinguished from the northern race by the triangular-shaped black notches on each belly scale. Throat color is carrot orange instead of red.

Stilosoma extenuatum Brown **Short-tailed Snake**

Description: This small, slender snake reaches a length of 20 inches (51 cm). The pencil-thick body is usually smoky gray with dark brown or black blotches down the center and on the sides. Some specimens have orange to dark red color between the dorsal blotches while others are gray. The top of the *very small blunt head* is dark brown or black. The eyes are small. The gray belly is heavily blotched with dark brown or black. The scales are smooth and glossy.

RAY E. ASHTON, JR.

orange-marked phase short-tailed snake

JOHN B. IVERSON

gray color phase short-tailed snake

The Snakes—Colubrids

Juveniles: Unknown, but probably like adults.

Similar Species: Juvenile racers and coachwhips have large eyes and a head that is much larger than the neck. The juvenile rat snakes also have relatively large heads and stocky bodies.

Natural History: This very secretive snake lives in the sandy soils of upland ridges and is most commonly found in longleaf pine-turkey oak habitats with

Range of the Short-tailed Snake in Florida. Insert map shows general distribution of the species in the United States.

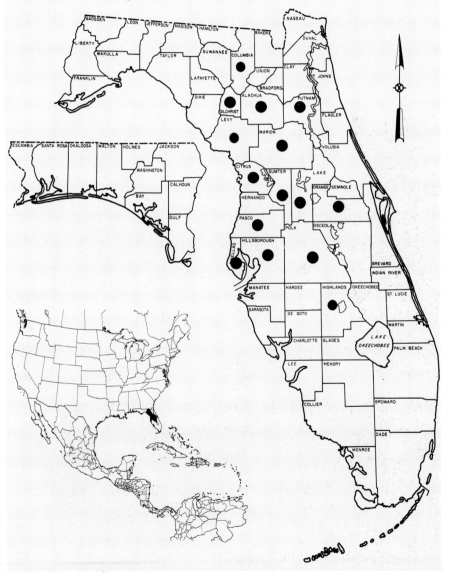

some specimens being found in xeric oak hammocks. Many specimens have been collected by people living in suburbs developed on these upland habitats. They are sometimes found in late fall under objects or in leaf litter. In captivity, the short-tailed snake will eat crowned snakes and occasionally ground skinks. So few specimens have been collected, and so few studies of this snake have been made, that we know very little about it. It seems to be a burrowing species, rarely coming to the surface. When alarmed, the snake will strike wildly and vibrate its tail. Some consider this species to be threatened; however, there is not enough known about the habits of distribution of this species to make such a decision.

Reproduction: Nothing is known about reproduction in this species except that it lays eggs, probably underground.

Storeria dekayi victa Hay **Florida Brown Snake**

Description: This small brown snake reaches a length of up to 19 inches (48 cm). The back is marked with 2 faint rows of small dark spots. The neck has two rings—one light ring just behind the head followed by a dark brown one. The head is small, about the same size as the neck, and the scales are keeled. The underside is tan to pink flesh colored with occasional dark flecks.

Juveniles: The young are similar to the adults, but are gray with a distinct light neck ring.

Similar Species: The redbelly snake had three or four faint dark stripes down the back. The underside is orange to red. Adult earth snakes lack rings on the neck and rows of spots on the back.

Natural History: The brown snake is common near aquatic habitats. It has been found in water hyacinths and in detritus at the water's edge in cypress heads. It is common in parks and around homes that are near ponds or drainage ditches. It feeds on earthworms, gastropods (slugs), small salamanders, and inverte-

ED CASSANO

Florida brown snake

The Snakes—Colubrids

brates. When first captured, this snake will flatten its body and strike repeatedly, but its head and teeth are too small to inflict even the slightest wound. After a short while, the brown snake will become tame and do well in captivity.

Reproduction: Breeding occurs from early spring through early summer. Three to 18 young are usually born in August to September, but some young may be born in the spring.

Range of the Florida Brown Snake in Florida. Marsh Brown Snake indicated by ● , Midland Brown Snake indicated by ☆ . Insert map shows general distribution of Brown Snakes in the United States.

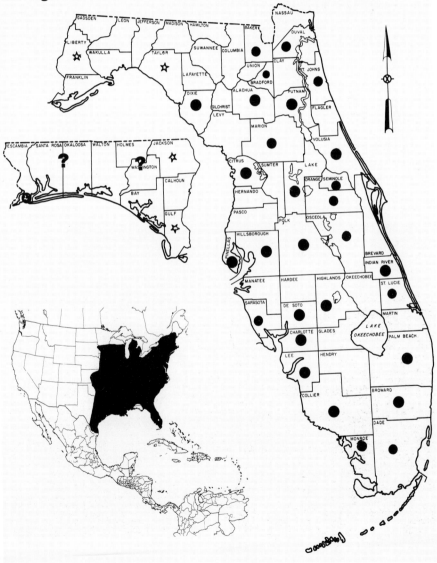

Subspecies:

Storeria dekayi wrightorum Trapido **Midland Brown Snake** This snake is similar to the Florida brown snake. It differs in that it has a faint light stripe down the center of the back. The faint dark spots are connected across the back by dark bars.

Storeria dekayi limnetes Anderson **Marsh Brown Snake** This subspecies is found only in the coastal marshes of Pensacola Bay. It lacks dark markings on the labial scales, but has horizontal dark bars across the temporal scales.

Storeria occipitomaculata obscura Trapido
Florida Redbelly Snake

Description: This colorful little snake may be slate gray, leaf brown, or rusty orange on the back. All color phases have 4 narrow dark brown stripes—two on the back and two on the sides. *The belly is bright orange, red or strawberry red with a row of dark spots on each side.* The head is small and usually brown. Most specimens have a light band or three light spots around the neck. The scales are keeled. It reaches a maximum length of 16 inches (40 cm).

JOHN B. IVERSON

Florida redbelly snake

The Snakes—Colubrids

Juveniles: The young are similar to adults.

Similar Species: The Florida brown snake, which is a close relative of the redbelly snake, differs by having two rows of spots down the back, and tan or flesh colored belly. The black swamp snake is plain black above.

Natural History: The redbelly snake is rarely encountered in Florida, due, in part, to its secretive habits. It occurs in mesic hammocks or damp woodlands, where it burrows through leaf mold and under rotting logs. Little is known about the Florida race, however, it probably feeds on small salamanders, gastropods (slugs), earthworms, and other invertebrates.

When alarmed, this snake will flatten itself almost to a ribbon thickness. Most specimens do not attempt to bite. Redbelly snakes do well in captivity if given a place to hide and earthworms to eat.

Reproduction: Little is known about the reproduction of this species in Florida. However, the author has collected juveniles in October and November, indicating that young are often born during middle to late summer. Other records show that young may also be born during the spring, indicating that breeding may take place in the fall. Eight to 20 young may be born at any one time.

Subspecies: *Storeria o. occipitomaculata* (Storer) **Northern Redbelly Snake** Intergrades between this race and the Florida redbelly snake are found in the panhandle. This race is distinguished by light white spots on the neck, and the sides of the head are black.

J. ERIC JUTERBOCK

northern redbelly snake

The Snakes—Colubrids

Range of the Florida Redbelly Snake in Florida is designated by the open area, Northern Redbelly Snake by the :::: area. Insert map shows general distribution of the species in the United States.

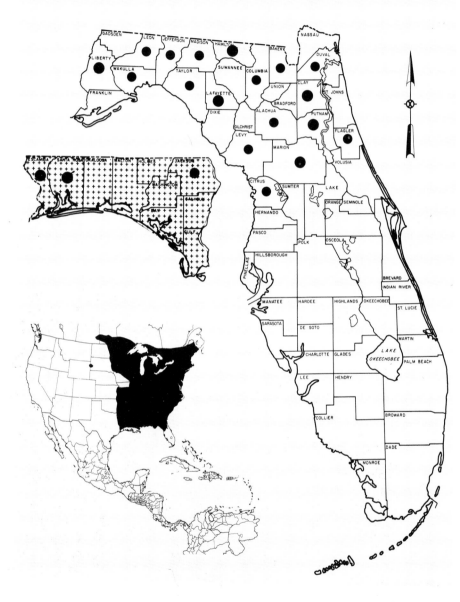

The Snakes—Colubrids

Tantilla coronata   Baird and Girard
Southeastern Crowned Snake

Description: This tiny snake is uniformly brown on the back with a black head and collar, separated by a light band. The underside is tan, brown, or pinkish. The scales are smooth and glossy. Maximum length is 13 inches (33 cm).

Juveniles: The young are similar to adults.

Similar Species: Ringneck snakes have bright yellow bellies and gray backs.

Natural History: The crowned snake, named for its black head, is locally common. It is found in dry, sandy habitats such as exist in xeric oak and upland pine habitats. Often this tiny snake is under debris, leaf litter, and logs. Most of its life is spent underground where it apparently eats termites and other invertebrates. The crowned snake is commonly eaten by scarlet kingsnakes and coral snakes.

This species does not do well in captivity. They will survive for some time if placed in a container of damp sand and fed live termites, spiders, and small centipedes.

Reproduction: Breeding probably occurs in the early spring. Eggs are small, white, and oval, usually three or less per clutch. They probably are laid underground and under logs or bark.

JACK DERMID

southeastern crowned snake

Range of the Southeastern Crowned Snake in Florida. Insert map shows general distribution of the species in the United States.

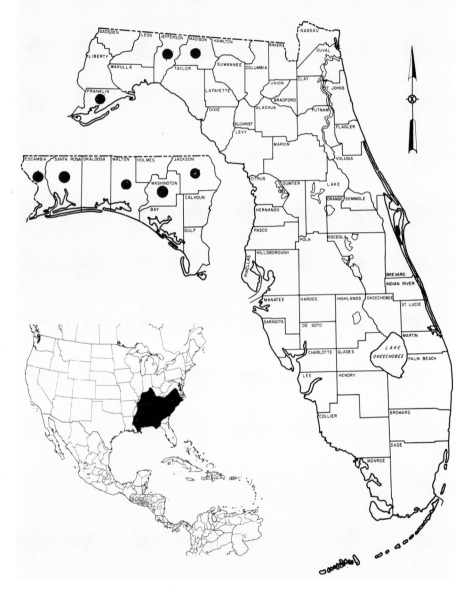

The Snakes—Colubrids

southeastern crowned snake   peninsula crowned snake

Florida crowned snake   coastal dunes crowned snake   rim rock crowned snake

Tantilla relicta relicta   Telford   **Penisula Crowned Snake**

Description: This snake is generally tan to light brown. The scales are smooth and glossy. The black on the head extends down to the edge of the lip and onto the nape. There is a light ring around the neck; head is narrow and pointed. and the snout projects beyond the lower jaw. This small, thin snake has a flesh-colored belly and reaches a length of 9 inches (23 cm).

The Snakes—Colubrids

Juveniles: The young are similar to adults.

Similar Species: Ringneck snakes have a bright yellow to orange belly. The easiest way to distinguish the different species and subspecies of crowned snakes is by the type of habitat and geographic location in which they are found.

Natural History: The peninsula crowned snake is restricted to scrub habitats and sandhills. It also occurs in coastal scrub habitats in Charlotte, Sarasota, Pinellas, and Levy counties.

Very little is known about any of the crowned snakes. They are very secretive and spend much time under the surface of the soil or hidden under leaf litter, bark, or logs. Presumably, they feed on termites and other invertebrates.

Reproduction: Breeding habits probably are similar to those of the southeastern crowned snake.

J. ERIC JUTERBOCK

peninsula crowned snake

LOUIS PORRAS

Florida crowned snake

The Snakes—Colubrids

Subspecies:

Tantilla relicta neilli Telford **Florida Crowned Snake** Unlike other crowned snakes, this race lacks a neck band. It is found in sandhill and mesic habitats of north-central Florida.

Tantilla relicta pamlica Telford **Coastal Dunes Crowned Snake** This subspecies has a broad band around the neck and some white flecking on the snout. It occurs in isolated coastal dunes and scrub in southeastern Florida including Cape Canaveral and Palm Beach County, west to the Kissimmee River.

Related Species: Tantilla oolitica Telford **Rim Rock Crowned Snake** This threatened species is the rarest snake in Florida and possibly the United States. Only a few have been collected. It occurs only in eastern Dade County where the oolitic limestone is near the surface, and on the upper Florida Keys, Monroe County. The specimens collected thus far have been taken near tropical hardwood hammocks. It resembles the southeastern crowned snake in appearance. The black on the head continues down onto the neck, and the snout

WILLIAM B. and KATHLEEN V. LOVE

coastal dunes crowned snake

LOUIS PORRAS

rim rock crowned snake

The Snakes—Colubrids

141

is tan. The Key Largo specimens may have a broken light band between the head and the neck. It is speculated that, like other crowned snakes, the rim rock crowned snake feeds on small centipedes.

Range of the Florida Crowned Snake is designated by the ▒ area, the Coastal Dunes Crowned Snake by the ⠿ area, and the ◑ indicates the Rim Rock Crowned Snake. The Peninsula Snake is found in the upland areas of the Central Ridge in marion, Charlotte, Sarasota, Pinellas, Levy, Polk, and Highlands counties. Insert map shows general distribution of *Tantilla relicta* **in the United States.**

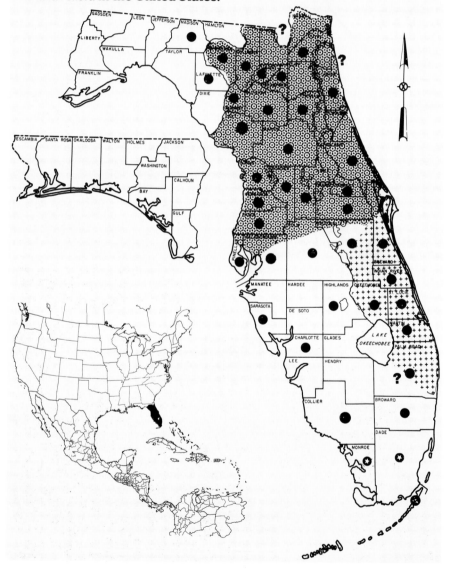

The Snakes—Colubrids

Thamnophis sauritus sackeni (Kennicott)
Peninsula Ribbon Snake

Description: This thin, long-tailed snake resembles the garter snake. It usually has three light stripes, *but the stripe down the center of the back may be faint or sometimes absent.* The stripes are yellowish to tan. The belly is yellowish white to tan. The head is small with a white spot in front of the eye and white or yellowish-white lips. It reaches a maximum length of 40 inches (101 cm).

Juveniles: Similar to adults.

Similar Species: Garter snakes have a prominent central stripe and lack the white spot in front of the eye. Garter snakes also have heavier bodies. The ribbon snake has a long, thin tail making up more than 25% of the total length.

Natural History: The ribbon snake is common in marshes, wet prairies and similar aquatic habitats. It is an excellent climber and is often found in low shrubs. It feeds on small fish, cricket and tree frogs. When captured, it rarely attempts to bite, but will release musk. The ribbon snake will remain nervous in captivity.

Reproduction: Breeding probably occurs in early spring. Three to 20 young are born in midsummer.

Subspecies:

Thamnophis sauritus sauritus (Linnaeus) **Eastern Ribbon Snake** This subspecies is found in north Florida and has a bright yellow central stripe.

Thamnophis sauritus nitae Rossman **Bluestripe Ribbon Snake** The central stripe is lacking and the stripes on the sides are blue to white. The back is black or chocolate brown, the underside is blue. This race is only found in the big bend country of the Gulf Coast.

WILLIAM B. and KATHLEEN V. LOVE

peninsula ribbon snake

Range of the Peninsula Ribbon Snake in Florida is designated by the open area, Bluestripe Ribbon Snake by the \\\ area, Eastern Ribbon Snake by the ⁞⁞⁞ area. Insert map show general distribution of the species in the United States.

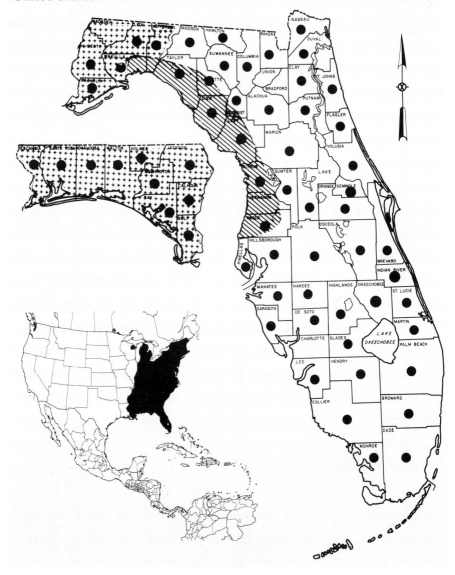

⬿ The Snakes—Colubrids

bluestripe ribbon snake

eastern ribbon snake

The Snakes—Colubrids

Thamnophis sirtalis sirtalis (Linnaeus)
Eastern Garter Snake

Description: Highly variable in color, the garter snake, however, in all color variations, has three wide light stripes down the back. These stripes may be yellow to yellow brown or the center stripe may be bluish. The dorsal background color may be a dark brown to light brown. It may also have the appearance of being blotched. Skin between the scales may be yellowish, reddish orange or bluish. The underside is bluish gray or bluish green. All belly scales are marked with a black spot on each side. Garter snakes reach a maximum length of 48 inches (122 cm).

Juveniles: Similar to adults.

JOSEPH T. COLLINS

eastern garter snake

JOHN B. IVERSON

bluestripe garter snake

146   The Snakes—Colubrids

Similar Species: Ribbon snakes are similar to garter snakes, even more so to the young who are usually thin bodied. Ribbon snakes have narrow pointed heads marked with bright white lines in front of the eye and around the mouth. Also, the tails of ribbon snakes are long. The central dorsal stripe in Florida ribbon snakes (except in northwest Florida) is dull, almost absent.

Range of the Eastern Garter Snake in Florida is designated by the open area, Bluestripe Garter Snake by the ⠿ area. Insert map shows general distribution of the species in the United States.

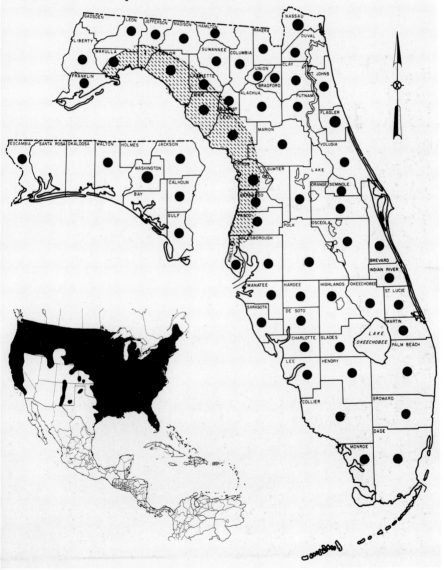

Natural History: The garter snake occurs in a wide variety of habitats, but it is most commmon near aquatic environments. It prefers small frogs and toads, but also eats minnows, salamanders and earthworms, and larger individuals will eat small rodents and even other snakes.

When cornered, the garter snake will flatten its head and body, expel musk, and bite. Garter snakes make excellent captives.

Reproduction: The garter snake is one of the champions in producing young. Up to 80 young may be born at one time, but the average number per litter is about 20. Young are usually born in middle to late summer, but spring broods have been recorded.

Subspecies: *Thamnophis sirtalis similis* Rossman **Bluestripe Garter Snake** The center stripe is dull tan and the stripes on the sides are blue. This subspecies is often confused with the bluestripe ribbon snake. This garter snake is confined to the big bend areas of the west central Gulf coast.

Virginia striatula (Linnaeus) **Rough Earth Snake**

Description: This small snake, which reaches a length of 12½ inches (32 cm), is brown to gray brown on the back and cream to yellow on the belly. There may be a light faint ring around the neck in some individuals. The head is small with a pointed snout. The keeled scales are small and glossy.

Juveniles: Similar to adults, but a white neck ring may be clearly present.

Similar Species: The smooth earth snake has a rounded snout and smooth scales. The pinewoods snake has a dark line from the mouth through the eye, and has smooth scales.

Natural History: This uncommon snake is found only in the northern part of the state. It lives in the drier hammocks and pine flatwoods, and is found under objects in much drier habitats than the smooth earth snake. They are most commonly collected under flat objects in trash piles. The rough earth snake feeds

JACK DERMID

rough earth snake

148   The Snakes—Colubrids

primarily on invertebrates. The author has collected several individuals at the edge of ant colonies, near the cocoons and larvae, indicating that these may be taken for food. Small lizards such as the ground skink and small frogs have also been reported as food for this species. Although quite docile, this secretive snake does not do well in captivity.

Reproduction: Two or three young per litter are born in summer.

Range of the Rough Earth Snake in Florida. Insert map shows general distribution of the species in the United States.

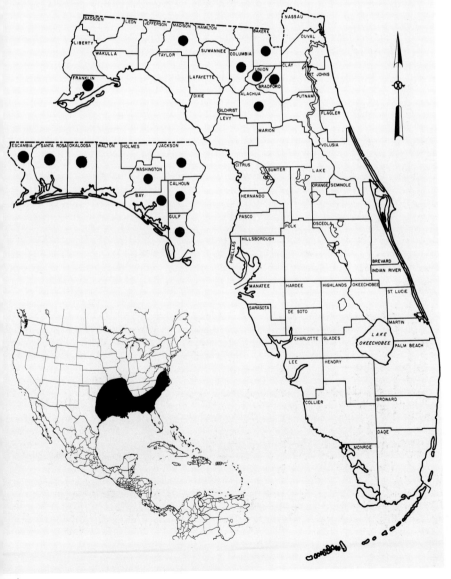

Virginia valeriae valeriae (Baird and Girard)
Smooth Earth Snake

Description: This little snake is brown above with very faint dark flecks or blotches. The belly is plain tan of cream; head is small and pointed; scales are usually smooth. The smooth earth snake reaches a maximum size of 12.6 inches (32 cm).

Juveniles: Similar to adults.

Similar Species: The rough earth snake has keeled scales. The pine woods snake has a dark line from the snout through the eye.

Natural History: The smooth earth snake is apparently rare in Florida. It inhabits mesic hammocks and wooded areas around marshes and other damp places. It feeds primarily on earthworms, snails, and other invertebrates. Little is known of its habits in Florida. This species does not do well in captivity.

Reproduction: Seven to 10 young are probably born during summer.

JOHN B. IVERSON

smooth earth snake

The Snakes—Colubrids

Range of the Smooth Earth Snake in Florida. Insert map shows general distribution of the species in the United States.

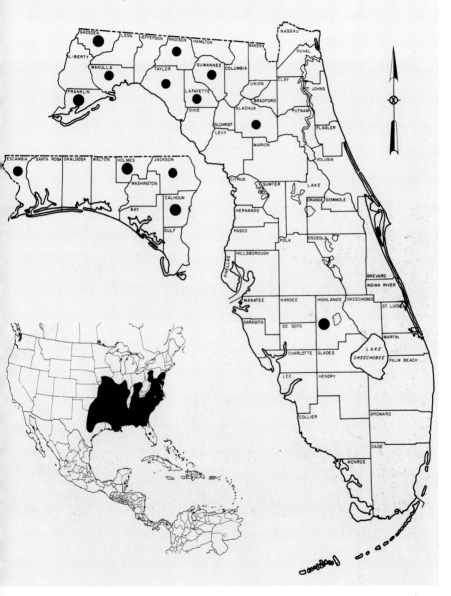

☠ *Micrurus fulvius fulvius* (Linnaeus) **Eastern Coral Snake**

Description: The average size is under 30 inches (76 cm), but the coral snake may reach a length of 47½ inches (120 cm). This beautiful snake has a *black snout,* a broad yellow band across the back of the head and neck, and a body pattern of black and red bands separated by narrow yellow rings. The red bands are often heavily flecked with black. The scales are smooth and glossy.

Juveniles: Similar to adults.

eastern coral snake

color variant found in southern Florida

The Snakes—Elapids

Similar Species: The scarlet kingsnake has a pointed red snout and broad red body bands bordered by thin black bands. Scarlet snakes have a white belly.

Natural History: The coral snake is quite common in some areas, but secretive habits cause it to be rarely seen. It is found in most habitats but probably is most common along the edges of woodlands and wet areas. This snake is occasionally found in yards by persons raking leaves or moving wood piles. Coral snakes are observed most often in the fall and spring, possibly due to a period of high activity in this species. Many people have many misconceptions about the coral snake. It is true that small coral snakes must chew to inject venom from relatively small, straight fangs that are fixed in the front of the mouth. However, larger coral snakes have larger mouths and very respectable fangs, quite capable of inflicting a serious bite immediately. Never handle this potentially dangerous animal. Its neurotoxic venom is quite deadly, but death rarely, if ever, occurs in a few moments after a bite, nor is it imminent. Antivenin and other medical procedures have been developed to counteract the effects of coral snake venom.

Reproduction: Breeding takes place in the fall and spring. Up to 7 long white eggs are laid, probably underground, during May or June. Eggs hatch in late summer or early fall.

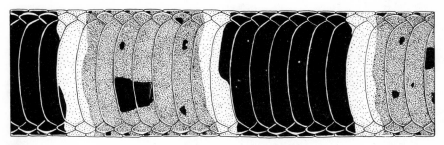

belly pattern—eastern coral snake

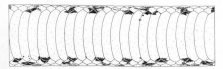

belly pattern—scarlet snake

belly pattern—scarlet kingsnake

Range of the Eastern Coral Snake in Florida. Insert map shows general distribution of the species in the United States.

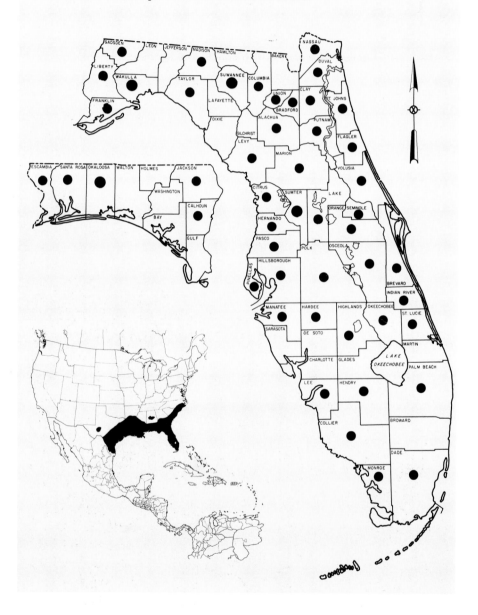

The Snakes—Elapids

🛇 *Agkistrodon contortrix contortrix* (Linnaeus)
Southern Copperhead

Description: The copperhead can attain a maximum length of 52 inches (132 cm), but adults usually average less than 34 inches (85 cm). The moderately broad head is tan to golden brown. Usually there are two small, dark, round spots in the center of the head between the eyes. The pupils are elliptical, and there is a large pit between the nostril and eye. The roughly scaled back is banded with broad alternating light and dark brown bands. The light bands are faintly bordered with white or cream. The belly is mottled with rich chocolate brown.

Juveniles: Similar to adults but with a yellow to yellow-green tail.

Similar Species: The cottonmouth has a much broader, thicker head with light stripes above the mouth. Also, most adult cottonmouths have obscure patterns.

Natural History: The copperhead is only found in the panhandle, particularly in Gadsden and Liberty counties. It is most common in wooded areas near water. It is often found under debris around old buildings. Copperheads are not uncommon around houses in the suburbs. A rather docile nocturnal snake, the copperhead rarely bites unless stepped on or touched. The camouflaged copper-colored snake will simply be still in the middle of a well-used path while scores of people unknowingly walk around or over it. The copperhead feeds on lizards, frogs, insects, and small mammals. The smell of the copperhead's musk is

R.W. VAN DEVENDER

juvenile southern copperhead—note yellow tail

The Snakes—Viperids   155

quite distinctive and can occasionally be recognized while walking in the woods, even though no snake is in sight. The bite of the copperhead, although usually much less severe than the cottonmouth, is dangerous and should receive medical attention.

Reproduction: Breeding occurs in the early spring, soon after the snakes emerge from hibernation. In the late summer, 5 to 6 young are born.

Range of the Southern Copperhead in Florida. Insert map shows general distribution of the species in the United States.

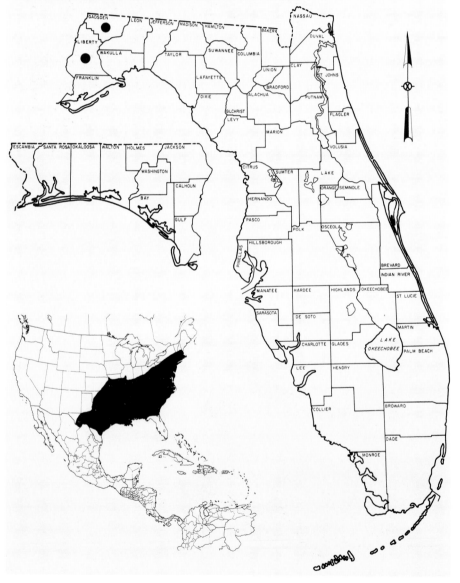

The Snakes—Viperids

adult southern copperhead

live birth—copperhead
emerging from membrane

The Snakes—Viperids

♨ *Agkistrodon piscivorus conanti*   Gloyd
Florida Cottonmouth

Description: This species reaches a maximum length of 74 inches (188 cm), but average about 36 inches (91 cm). The thick head is lance shaped and much larger than the neck. The top of the head is black to dark brown. *The edges of the mouth are light tan or creamy white.* The rough scaled back is black to rich brown

Note light edges along lips and pit of Florida cottonmouth.

Florida cottonmouth

The Snakes—Viperids

with broad faint bands. The belly is cream white mottled with black or reddish brown blotches. The pupils are elliptical. There is a deep pit between the nostril and eye.

Juveniles: Newborn cottonmouths resemble copperheads. They are banded with light and dark brown and are generally much lighter in color than the adults. The tails of juveniles are sulfur yellow to light green in color.

Range of the Cottonmouth in Florida. Insert map shows general distribution of the species in the United States.

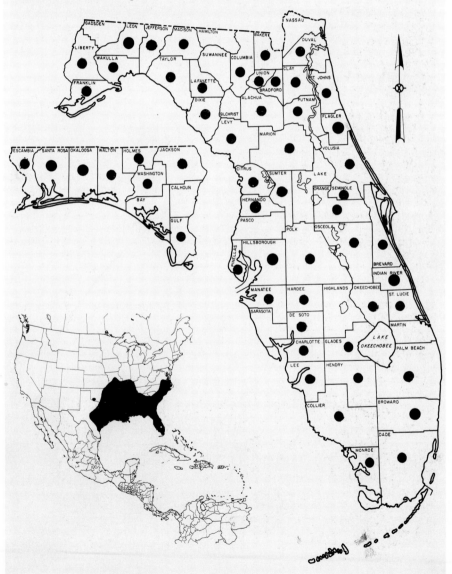

juvenile Florida cottonmouth

Similar Species: The copperhead lacks striping on the sides of the head, and it has distinct light and dark brown bands on the back. All water snakes may flatten their heads when alarmed, but their heads never appear to be as thick and bulky as the cottonmouth. The nonpoisonous water snakes have spots or narrow bands across the back. Also, the water snakes have round pupils and divided scales on the underside of the tail, which are not found on the cottonmouth.

Natural History: The cottonmouth is one of the most common poisonous snakes in Florida. More often than not, however, nonpoisonous water snakes are confused with cottonmouths. When alarmed, a cottonmouth gapes its mouth and exposes its curved fangs. Cottonmouths rarely bite unless provoked or stepped on. The bite should be considered dangerous, often causing serious tissue damage and occasionally being fatal.

Cottonmouths eat almost any animal small enough for them to swallow. Fish, other snakes, young turtles, baby alligators, amphibians, small mammals, and various invertebrates are included in their diet. The young use the colored tail as a lure to attract frogs to within striking range.

Ponds and streams in pine flatwoods are the prime habitat for this species, but they are found around any freshwater habitats in the state. They also are common on many offshore keys.

Reproduction: Mating apparently occurs throughout the year. As many as 12 young are born, usually during summer. Females apparently produce a litter every other year.

160   The Snakes—Viperids

☠ *Crotalus adamanteus*   Beauvois
Eastern Diamondback Rattlesnake

Description: Among the largest North American snakes, the diamondback has a record length of 96 inches (244 cm). The average length is under 71 inches (180 cm). Its body is extemely bulky and the head is quite large. The smoky gray, rough-scaled back has broad, dark brown, *diamond shaped blotches bordered with thin bands of black and white.* The tail is banded with dark rings. The head is striped on its sides with black and white and has a large pit between the nostril and eye. The tail ends in a well developed rattle.

Juveniles: Similar to adults, but with only a small button on the tail tip.

Similar Species: The timber rattlesnake lacks white stripes and tail bands. The pigmy rattlesnake is blotched and lacks the diamonds on the back.

Natural History: This magnificent reptile, once common in most of the state, continues to decline at an alarming rate. This is due primarily to habitat destruction from land development, lumbering practices, and the decline of gopher tortoise populations. It commonly inhabits palmetto pine flatwoods, at the edge of wet savannas. It feeds primarily on small mammals, from mice to rabbits. The diamondback will often remain motionless in the shadows of the undergrowth until it is disturbed. When alarmed, it will coil, raising the anterior half of the body far above the ground in an S-shaped striking pose. The well developed rattle can be heard for a long distance. The strike can reach at least one-third the total length of the snake. Its fangs are extremely well developed and can penetrate through clothing and thin shoes. The diamondback should be treated with great respect and not contempt.

Commercial rattlesnake roundups are held in various areas of the state. During these events, participants use gasoline to flush wintering snakes from

JIM BRIDGES

eastern diamondback rattlesnake

gopher tortoise burrows. This practice not only has greatly depleted the ecologically valuable rattlesnake population but it has also destroyed numerous other animals including the threatened indigo snake. This practice is now illegal in Florida.

Reproduction: Breeding probably occurs in the late fall and spring. Between 8-15 young are born in late summer or early fall. The young are nearly 12 inches long at birth.

Range of the Eastern Diamondback Rattlesnake in Florida. Insert map shows general distribution of the species in the United States.

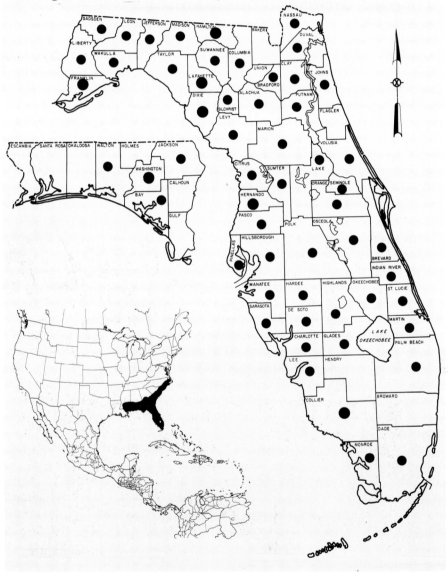

The Snakes—Viperids

🐍 *Crotalus horridus* (Linnaeus)
Timber Rattlesnake, Canebrake Rattlesnake

Description: The average length of this species is approximately 52 inches (130 cm), but it may reach a record length of 74½ inches (188 cm). The head and rough-scaled back are pinkish gray to gray brown to chocolate brown or black on the tail. *The back is crossed by dark brown to black zigzag chevrons.* There is a rusty red stripe down the center of the back. The pupils are vertical, and there is a pit between the nostril and the eye.

Juveniles: Similar to adults. The tail ends in a button.

Similar Species: The pigmy rattlesnake is spotted. The diamondback has well defined diamond shaped markings along the back.

Natural History: The canebrake was once considered a separate race from the timber rattlesnake. The two occur in different habitats, the timber being an upland form, while the canebrake inhabits wet lowland forests. The canebrake is found in wet pine flatwoods, river bottoms and hydric hammocks of the northern counties, where it may be common. It feeds on small rodents, rabbits, and occasionally birds. Unlike the diamondback, it has a relatively mild disposition and will sit quietly coiled if left undisturbed. However, if disturbed, it can inflict a serious, potentially fatal bite. Little is known about the habits of this species in Florida.

Reproduction: As many as 12 young are born during late summer.

ED CASSANO

timber rattlesnake

Range of the Timber Rattlesnake (Canebrake Rattlesnake) in Florida. Insert map shows general distribution of the species in the United States.

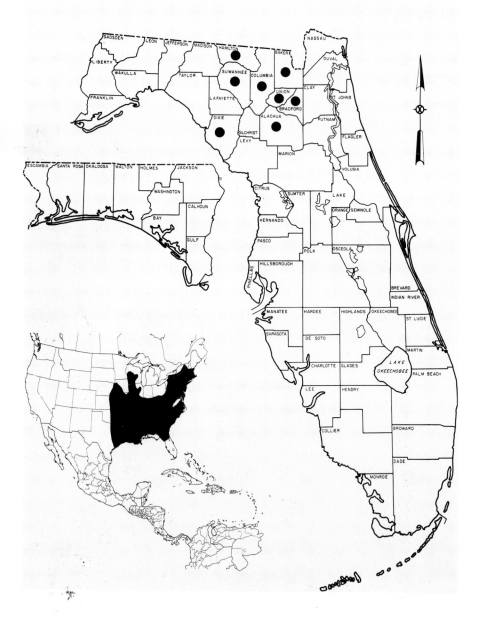

The Snakes—Viperids

☠ *Sistrurus miliarius barbouri*   Gloyd
Dusky Pigmy Rattlesnake

Description: This small rattlesnake attains a record length of 31 inches (79 cm) but adults average 20 inches (51 cm). The rough-scaled gray back *has a row of prominent large circular spots down its center and a faint row of similar spots on either side.* The spots are bordered by a thin light ring. The tail ends in a small delicate rattle and is usually banded. Pupils are vertical and there is a pit between the nostril and eye on each side of the broad head. The belly is light gray with scattered large, dark blotches.

Juveniles: Similar to adults except the tail ends in a button.

Similar Species: The hognose snakes, especially the gray color phases, may sometimes be mistaken for the pigmy rattler. The rattle and vertical pupils are distinctive in the pigmy.

Natural History: This relatively common rattlesnake occurs in assorted Florida habitats, but it is most common in pine flatwoods, scrub, or longleaf pine habitats near water. It feeds on insects and small vertebrates including frogs, lizards, and mice. The pigmy is quite pugnacious in nature and often bites at the slightest provocation. Many more people would be killed by snake bite every year if the diamondback had the same temperament as the pigmy. The pigmy reportedly has potent venom, but its small size, its small fangs, and the amount of venom released usually make the bite less serious than that of the other

JIM BRIDGES

dusky pigmy rattlesnake

poisonous snakes in Florida. When disturbed, the pigmy may not rattle. The rattle sounds more like an insect singing than that of the rattle of a rattlesnake.

Pigmy rattlesnakes are seen most frequently crossing roads at dusk or early evening, particularly in the fall.

Reproduction: Seven to 9 young are born during late summer. Little is known about reproduction in this species.

Range of the Dusky Pigmy Rattlesnake in Florida. Insert map shows general distribution of the species in the United States.

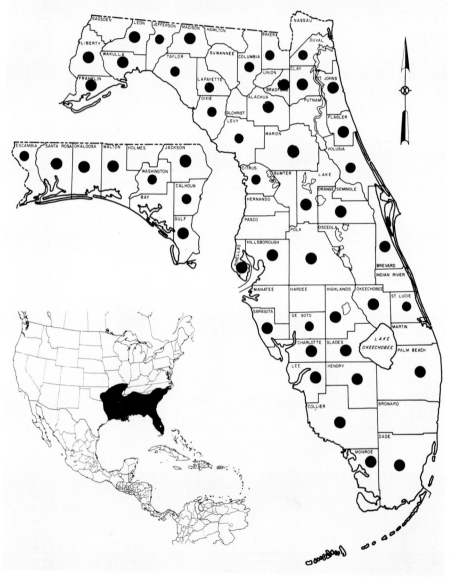

The Snakes—Viperids

GLOSSARY

anal scale (plate)   the scale covering the anus or cloacal opening in some lizards and all snakes. This scale marks the beginning of the tail.

anterior   front or head end

back   the upper or dorsal area of the body, along either side of the backbone

band   a marking or wide stripe that is different from the background color and crosses over the back

belly   the under or ventral side of the body

blotch   a large spot, irregular but circular marking

body groove   a lengthwise fold in the body surface

cloaca   the common opening of the reproductive, urinary, and disgestive systems that terminates at the anal opening

collar   a band of color across the neck, just behind the head

diurnal   active during the daytime

dorsal (dorsum)   upper surface or back of the animal

dorsolateral   the region between the back and sides of the body

endemic   restricted to a limited area

flecks   small irregularly shaped "chips" or dots of color

fossorial (animal)   a burrowing animal

frontal   large scale on the top of the head between the eyes

hammock   *See habitat descriptions.*

herpetology   the study of amphibians and reptiles

hydric   wet, swampy. *See habitat descriptions.*

keeled   with a ridge, usually along the center, like the keel on a boat; refers to scales of some snakes and lizards

labials   scales on the upper and lower lips

larvae   an aquatic pre-adult stage which possesses feathery-like gills in salamanders. Tadpoles are larval frogs or toads.

longitudinal   extending along the length

mesic   moist but not swampy. *See habitat descriptions.*

middorsal   located in the middle of the back

nasals   the scales in which the nostrils are located

nocturnal   active during the night

ovoid   shaped like a chicken egg

pit   the triangular shaped hole between and below the nostril and eye of pit-vipers

posterior   rear or tail end

postlabials   scales posterior to the upper labials

post oculars   the scales directly behind the eye

race subspecies or geographic color variations

reticulated having a network of lines forming an irregular web-like pattern

ring a broad stripe completely encircling the body

saddle a large blotch reaching across the back and onto the sides

scute a large, plate-like scale

snout the part of the head anterior to the eyes

snout-vent length the distance from tip of the snout to the anterior lip of the vent

supraocular those scales along dorsal margin of the eye

tail length the distance from the anterior lip of the vent to the top of the tail

upper labials scales along the upper lip except on the end of the snout (rostral)

ventrals belly plates from neck to anal plate

Scale Patterns

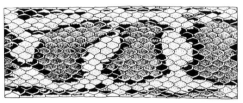

blotched

saddle or diamond

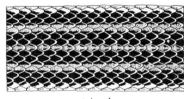

striped

Scale Types

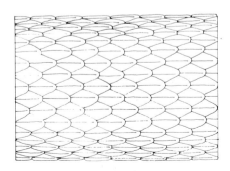

keeled

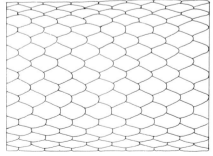

smooth

Scale Types

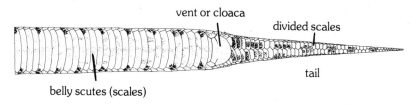

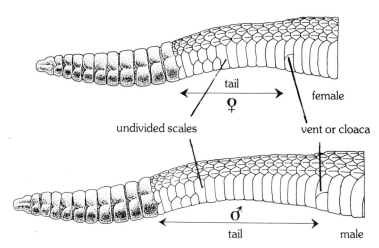

Scale Identification

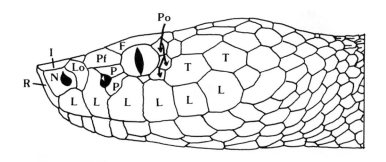

I = internasal   **Pf** = prefrontal
R = rostral   **P** = preocular
N = nasal   **F** = frontal
Lo = lorial   **Po** = postocular
L = labial   **T** = temporal

Glossary

BIBLIOGRAPHY

The bibliography consists of popular and scientific works that were used during the preparation of this book or are recommended references for schools and amateur herpetologists. The latter are indicated by *.

GENERAL REFERENCES ON REPTILES AND AMPHIBIANS

*ASHTON, Ray E., Jr. (Compiler). 1976. Endangered and threatened amphibians and reptiles in the United States. SSAR Misc. Publication, Herp. Circ. No. 5. 65 pp.

*ASHTON, Ray E., Jr. 1977. Identification manual to the reptiles and amphibians in Florida. Florida State Museum, Publ. Series, No. 1. 65 pp.

BEHLER, John L. and F. Wayne King. 1979. The Audobon Society field guide to North American reptiles and amphibians. Alfred A. Knopf, N.Y. 719 pp.

*BOWLER, Kevin J. 1977. Longevity of reptiles and amphibians in North American collections. SSAR Misc. Publ., Herp. Circ. No. 6. 32pp.

*CARR, Archie F. 1940. A contribution to the herpetology of Florida. Univ. Fla., Publ-Biol. Sc. Series, III (1).

*CARR, Archie F., and Coleman Goin. 1955. Guide to the reptiles, amphibians and fresh-water fishes of Florida. Univ. Florida Press, Gainesville, Florida 341 pp.

COCHRAN, Doris M. 1970. The new general field book of reptiles and amphibians. G. P. Putman's Sons. N.Y.

COLLINS, Joseph T. (Chairman). Standard common and current scientific names for North American amphibians and reptiles. SSAR Misc. Publ. Herp. Circ. No. 7. 36 pp.

*CONANT, Roger. 1975. A field guide to reptiles and amphibians of eastern and central North America. 2nd edition. Houghton Mifflin Co., 429 pp.

*DUELLMAN, W. E., and A. Schwartz. 1958. Amphibians and reptiles of southern Florida. Bull. Fla. State. Mus. Biol. Sc. Ser. 324-361.

FERNER, John W. 1979. A review of marking techniques for amphibians and reptiles. SSAR Misc. Publ. Herp. Circ. No. 9. 41 pp.

*McDIARMID, Roy W. (Editor). 1978. Rare and endangered biota of Florida. Vol. 3. Amphibians and reptiles. University Presses of Florida, Gainesville. 74 pp.

MOUNT, Robert H. 1975. The reptiles and amphibians of Alabama. Agriculture Experiment Station, Auburn Univ. 347 pp.

*OULAHAN, Richard. 1976. Reptiles and amphibians. Time-Life Films, Inc. N.Y. 128 pp.

*PISANI, George R. 1973. A guide to preservation techniques for amphibians and reptiles. SSAR Misc. Publ., Herp. Circ., No. 1. 22 pp.

GENERAL-REPTILES

*ARNOLD, Robert E. 1973. What to do about bites and stings of venomous animals. The Macmillan Co., N.Y. 122 pp.

BELLAIRS, Angus. 1970. The life of reptiles. Universe Books, N.Y. 2 Volumes. 590 pp.

BELLAIRS, Angus and Richard Carrington. 1966. The world of reptiles. American Elsevier Publ. Co., Inc., N.Y.

BOGERT, Charles M. 1959. How reptiles regulate their body temperature. Scientific American 200:105-120.

*CARR, Archie. 1967. The reptiles: young reader's edition. Time-Life Books, Inc., N.Y.

FITCH, Henry S. 1970. Reproductive cycles of lizards and snakes. Museum of Natural History, University of Kansas, Lawrence, Kansas.

FRYE, Fredrick L. 1973. Husbandry, medicine and surgery in captive reptiles. VM Publishing Co., Bonner Springs, Kansas.

GOIN, Coleman J. and Olive B. Goin. 1962. Introduction to herpetology. W. H. Freeman Co., San Francisco.

*LANWORN, R. A. 1972. The book of reptiles. The Hamlyn Publishing Group, Ltd., N.Y.

*MINTON, Sherman H., Jr. and Madge R. Minton. 1969. Venomous reptiles. Weidenfeld and Nicolson, London.

MURPHY, James B. 1975. A brief outline of suggested treatments for diseases of captive reptiles. SSAR Misc. Pub. Herp. Circ., (4):13 pp.

*SCHMIDT, Karl P. and Robert F. Inger. 1957. Living reptiles of the world. Doubleday and Co., N.Y.

VAN MIEROP, L. H. S. 1976. Snakebite symposium. Journal Fla. Med. Assoc., 63(3):191-210.

SNAKES

AUFFENBERG, W. 1955. A reconsideration of the racer Coluber constrictor in eastern United States. Tulane Stud. Zool., 2:89-155.

BLANCHARD, F. N. 1923. The snakes of the genus Virginia. Publ. Mich. Acad. Sci., 3:343-365.

BLANCHARD, F. N. 1938. The ring-necked snakes of the genus Diadophis. Bull. Chicago Acad. Sc., 7:1-144.

BLANCHARD, F. N. 1938. Snakes of the genus Tantilla in the United States. Field Mus. Nat. Hist. Zool. Ser., 10:369-376.

BLANEY, Richard M. 1977. Systematics of the common kingsnake Lampropeltis getulus (Linnaeus). Tulane Studies in Zoology and Botany. Vol. 19 No. 3-4:47-103.

BURKETT, R. D. 1966. Natural history of the cottonmouth moccasin, Agkistrodon pisciviorus (Reptilia). Univ. Kansas Pub. Mus. Nat. Hist., 17:435-491.

CARR, Archie F., Jr. 1934. Notes on the habits of the short-tailed snake. Copeia (2):138-139.

CONANT, R. 1949. Two new races of Natrix erythrogaster. Copeia 1949. 1-15.

*CURRAN, C. H. and Carl Kauffeld. 1937. Snakes and their ways. Harper and Brothers, N.Y.

DOWLING, H. G. 1950. Studies of the black swamp snake, Seminatrix pygaea (Cope) with descriptions of two new subspecies. Misc. Pub. Mus. Zool. Univ. Mich., (76):1-38.

EOGREN, R. A. 1955. The natural history of the hog-nosed snakes, genus Heterodon: a review. Herpetologica 11:115-117.

FITCH, Henry S. 1960. Autecology of the copperhead. Univ. Kansas Pub. Mus. Nat. Hist., 13(4):85-288.

FRANZ, Richard. 1977. Observations of the food, feeding, behavior and parasites of the striped swamp snake, Regina alleni. Herpetologica 33:91-94.

GIBBONS, Whitfield J., John W. Coker and Thomas M. Murphy, Jr. 1977. Selected Aspects of the life history of the rainbow snake (Farancia erytrogramma). Herpetologica 33:276-281.

*HARRISON, Hal H. 1971. The world of the snake. J. B. Lippincott Co., N.Y. 156 pp.

HIGHTON, Richard. 1956. Systematics and variations of the endemic Florida snake genus, Stilosoma. Bull. Florida State Mus., 1(2):73-96.

*HYLANDER, C. J. 1951. Adventures with reptiles, the story of Ross Allen. Julian Messner, Inc. N.Y.

IVERSON, John B. 1978. Reproductive notes on Florida snakes. Florida Scientist Vol. 41 (4):201-207.

*KAUFFELD, Carl. 1957. Snakes and snake hunting. Hanover House, Garden City, N.Y.

*KAUFFELD, Carl. 1969. Snakes: the keeper and the kept. Doubleday and Co., N.Y.

*KLAUBER, Laurence, M. 1972. Rattlesnakes: their habits, life histories and influence on mankind. 2nd ed. Univ. California Press, Berkeley. 2 volumes.

MYERS, Charles W. 1965. Biology of the ring-neck snake, Diadophis punctatus, in Florida. Bull. Florida State Mus., 10(2):43-90.

MYERS, Charles W. 1967. The pinewoods snake Rhadinaea flavilata (Cope). Bull. Florida State Mus. 2(2):50-97.

NEILL, W. T. 1947. Size and habits of the cottonmouth moccasin. Herpetologica 3:203-205.

NEILL, W. T. 1951. Notes on the natural history of certain North American snakes. Publ. Res. Div. Ross Allen's Rep. Instit., 1(5):47-60.

PALMER, W. M. 1970. Notes on the natural history of the scarlet snake, Cemophora coccinea copei Jan, in North Carolina. Herpetologica, 26:300-302.

PARKER, H. W. and A. Grandison. 1977. Snakes: a natural history. British Museum, London.

PLATT, D. R. 1969. Natural history of the hognose snakes, Heterodon platyrhinos and Heterodon nasicus. Univ. Kansas. Pub. Mus. Nat. Hist., 18:253-420.

PORRAS, Louis and Larry David Wilson. 1979. New distributional records for Tantilla oolitica Telford (Reptilia, Serpentes, Colubridae) from the Florida Keys. Journal of Herp. Vol 13. No. 2. 218-220.

ROSSMAN, D. A. 1956. Notes on food of a captive black swamp snake, Seminatrix pygaea pygaea (Cope). Herpetologica, 12:154-155.

Bibliography   171

ROSSMAN, Douglas A. 1963. The colubrid snake genus *Thamnophis* a revision of the Sauritus group. Bull. Florida State Mus., 7(3):99-178.

ROSSMAN, D. A. 1970. *Thamnophis sauritus*. Cat. Amer. Amphib. Rept. 99.1-99.2.

SCHMIDT, Karl P. and D. Dwight Davis. 1941. Field book of snakes. G. P. Putnam's Sons N.Y. xiii & 365 pp.

TELFORD, Sam R., Jr. 1966. Variation among the southeastern crowned snakes, genus *Tantilla*. Bull. Florida State Mus., 10(7):261-304.

WHARTON, Charles H. 1969. The cottonmouth moccasin on Sea Horse Key, Florida. Bull. Florida State Mus., 14(3):227-272.

*WRIGHT, Albert H. and Anna A. Wright. 1957. Handbook of snakes of the United States and Canada. Comstock Publ. Assoc. 2 volumes.

FLORIDA HABITATS

BECK, William M., Jr. 1965. The streams of Florida. Bull. Florida St. Mus. 10 (3):91-126.

KERTZ, Herman. 1942. Florida dunes and scrub vegetation and geology. Florida Geol. Survey Bull., 23. 154 pp.

LAESSLE, A. M. 1942. The plant communities of the Welaka area. Univ. Florida Publ. Biol. Sci. Ser., 4(1):1-143.

LAESSLE, A. M. 1958. The origin and successional relationship of sandhill vegetation and sand-pine scrub. Ecol. Monogr. 28:361-387.

MONK, Carl D. 1960. A preliminary study on the relationships between the vegetation of a mesic hammock community and a sandhill community. Quart. Jour. Florida Acad. Sci., 23(1). 12 pp.

NEILL, Wilfred T. 1957. Historical biogeography of present-day Florida. Bull. Florida State Mus., 2(7):175-220.

YOUNG, Frank N. 1954. The water beetles of Florida. Univ. Florida Press, Biol. Sci. Series, 5(1). 238 pp.

INDEX

Numbers in parentheses ( ) refer to photos.

174

water oak   25
water snake, banded   103, 110
water snake, brown   112, (112)
water snake, Florida   106, (109), 115
water snake, Florida green   100, (101), 112, 113
water snake, glossy   120
water snake, midland   114, (114)
water snake, redbelly   103, (105), 104, 115

wax myrtle   24
white mangrove   16
wild celery   21
willow   25
winged elm   25
wire grass   24, (26)
xeric oak hammock   25, (26)
Yellow river   115

This book may be kept